THE COSTUMES AND
ADORNMENTS OF
CHINESE YI NATIONALITY
PICTURE ALBUM

Chief editor:
Shi Songshan (Yi)

Associate editors:
Zhang Fumin (Monggol), Jimubuchu (Yi), Zhao Yuchi

Editors:
(In the order of the strokes of the Chinese character)
Kuang Shizhao, Li Dan (Hui), He Yanwen,
Song Qinshi (Yi), Zheng Junxiu, Pu Zhangkai (Yi),
Xiong Meiliang (Yi)

Assistant editors:
(In the order of the strokes of the Chinese character)
Li Tiezhu, Zhong Xingkui (She), Yong Jirong (Qiang).

Photographers:
Long Guangmao (Miao), Jimubuchu (Yi),
Xiong Meiliang (Yi)
(The following is in the order of the number of
photos published:)
Gao Jingli, Yang Mishuang, Wu Shizhong,
He Yanwen, Zhang Danbo, Li Tiezhu,
Yang Guangquan, Leng Dengyi, Cen Shaoguang,
Yong Jirong, Zhao Yuchi, Hao Qingqi,
Tao Shuxiang, Sai Yunhe, Ma Yufu, Zhao Youxin,
Zhang Fumin, Bai Yingquang, Li Chengyong,
Wu Youcheng, Zheng Keguang, Su Futao,
Cai Jiansheng, Zhang Mengsheng, Sun Jun,
Zou Yongqiong, Su Cheng, She Mengliang,
Ma Changchun, Ma Shunrong

Adviser of designing:
Zhang Cizhong

Designers:
Yang Yizhong, Shi Lixing

Data collector:
Jiang Loxiang (Chaoxian)

Translators of English version:
Shen Shiguang, Zhou Ximin

Sketch of Yi population distribution:
Chen Yingchu, Zhao Hong

THE COSTUMES AND ADORNMENTS OF CHINESE YI NATIONALITY PICTURE ALBUM

CONTENTS

I warmly congratulate upon the publication of "The Costumes and Adornments of Chinese Yi Nationality Picture Album".

Yi Nationality is brave, industrious and full of creative power. Ancient Yi people who cultivated and herded in Jinsha River Valley and on Yunnan-Guizhou Plateau made great contribution to the development of southwest China and the formation and growth of a unified and multi-national country. The historical culture of Qiongdu, Yelang and Dianguo which was famous in ancient time contained the work and wisdom of ancient Yi people; the Nanzhao Country set up by the Mengs in the middle ancient times furthered the social development in southwest China. Yi writing characters have a long history known to the world. Yi people's creation and achievements embodied in science and technology, astronomy and calendar, philosophical thoughts as well as literature and art added dazzling brilliance to Chinese cultural treasure-house.

National costumes and adornments, a materialized spiritual product and an important inalienable part of national culture, present the history and the life of nationalities to the public. The most beautiful costumes and adornments of Yi people were and are a wonderful flower among various kinds of Chinese national costumes. Many styles of national costumes were lost during the changes of the times, sharing the same fate of other cultural heritage. National Cultural Palace and the departments concerned in Yunnan, Sichuan, Guizhou Provinces and Guangxi spared no efforts to study and sift the costumes and adornments of Yi Nationality, and held many exhibitions of the costumes and adornments of Yi Nationality in Beijing and Guizhou, Sichuan, Yunnan Provinces since the autumn of 1987. The exhibitions won enthusiastic approval from personalities of all nationalities and various circles as well as from foreign friends. "The Costumes and Adornments of Yi Nationality Picture Album" compiled and published on this basis provides valuable materials for the research on nationalities and social studies, and at the same time preserves the rich cultural heritage of Yi Nationality for the society and for descendants. I want to express my heartfelt thanks to the editors and publishers of the album who have done a significant and farsighted work.

The publication of the costumes and adornments of nationalities picture albums is an important work in national cultural construction. I have made a suggestion about the publication of series picture albums of 56 nationalities in our country. "The Costumes and Adornments of Miao Nationality Picture Album" has already come out. "The Costumes and Adornments of Yi Nationality Picture Album" is to be published soon. I hope that the picture albums of other nationalities will be compiled and published one after another. It is our belief that the publication of picture albums of the national costumes will be conductive to preserve and develop national cultural heritage, to further the understanding and friendship among nationalities home and abroad, and to promote the research on nationalities and social studies. Let's join our efforts to make the national costumes of our homeland more bright and colourful and socialist national culture more prosperous in the age of reform and opening to the outside world.

"The Costumes and Adornments of Chinese Yi Nationality Picture Album" is to present a rich and colourful costume world to the public.

The costumes and adornments of Yi Nationality are numerous in styles and rich in colours. There are different kinds of garments for male and female, for people of different ages, and gorgeous dress for festivals and common dress for daily wear. There are also wedding dress, mourning apparel, garments for sacrificial rites and clothing for war. In class society, the hierarchy was reflected in costumes and adornments. Historically, Yi Nationality was characterized by strong sense of patriarchal clan, numerous branches, vast area, complex natural environment and different productive economy patterns. These conditions together with the mutual effects between nationalities explained the distinct regional features of Yi people's costumes and adornments in materials, styles, ornaments and designs. Yi costumes are the mirror of Yi people's traditional features and also of the mutual effects and infiltration between the cultures of different nationalities.

This album divided the costumes and adornments of Yi Nationality into six models according to regional features and in the light of language distribution known as "social fossile": Liangshan, Wumeng Mountain, Honghe, southeast Yunnan Province, west Yunnan Province and Chuxiong. The models are subdivided into different styles, trying to make a relative complete and scientific research of the costume culture of Yi Nationality.

Daliangshan and Xiaoliangshan are one of the important regions where Yi Nationality live in compact cmmunities. Under slave-owning system for a long time, before the democratic reform in 1954, this region was extremely slow in the development of society. That is why this model of costumes and adornments which preserves many inherent cultural traditions is the most representative of Yi costumes.

Wumeng Mountain Region is one of the important regions inhabited by Yi Nationality since ancient time. This model of costumes is a distinct reflection of the inherent national tradition in this region and the obvious changes after the measures taken in the end of Ming Dynasty and at the beginning of Qing Dynasty "to replace hereditary headmen with officials".

In Honghe Region, the unbalanced development of economy and culture account for the numerous styles and brilliant colours of this model of costumes. Generally speaking, the costumes in secluded remote mountain area keep strong traditional characteristics, while in other regions, contacts among different nationalities make the costumes bear some similarities to those of Han people.

The unique features of the costumes in southeast Yunnan Province are embodied by distinct branch differences.

West Yunnan Province was the origin of ancient Nanzhao Country. The traces of gorgeous and richly decorated costumes worn by nobles of Nanzhao royal family can be found in women's festival dress.

Compared to other regions inhabited by Yi people, the region where the Chuxiong model of costumes prevails is the concentration area of various Yi branches, keeping the traditional culture of Yi Nationality. The development of economy and culture in the last 100 years brought about the changes in the costumes and adornments of Yi Nationality. Jackets with opening on the right side and trousers become the basic style of present time, while the old customs of wearing goat skin, clothes made of fire weed and collarless garments are more or less preserved until now.

Since Han Dynasty (206 B.C.— A.D.220), some customs of ancient Yi people recorded on cultural relics and in historical documents have been popular until now, reflecting the strong inheritance of Yi costumes. Yi people still wear goat skin, felt cape, collarless jacket and garment with long back hem. Women like to wear skirts while men are fond of wrapping the headscarf into a "Ziti" (hero knot).

Garments of Yi men in Daliangshan and Xiaoliangshan in Sichuan Province are alike to those of the images on the frescoes of the Huo's graveyard (386-394) built in East Jin Age which was discovered in Houhaizi of Zhaotong in Yunnan Province in 1963. Those images with their feet bare, wore felt capes and wrapped the headscarf into a "Ziti". This is the evidence of the long history of Yi costumes.

There is an account of the custom of wearing goat skin in "Man Shu" (book of Southern Nationalities) and other literature written by Fanchuo in Tang Dynasty (618-907). The custom still prevails in regions inhabited by Yi people. In Nanjian of Yunnan Province, brides have to wear goat skin at wedding whether their families are rich or poor. This custom shows how deep the influence of traditional customs and mentality is rooted in Yi people.

Collarless jacket is an ancient style in the developing process of costumes. According to the historical documents in Yuan Dynasty (1271-1368) and Ming Dynasty (1368-1644), ancient Yi women wore collarless jackets and skirts. This style of dress is still popular among Yi people in Chuxiong, Luquan, Honghe in Yunnan Province and Napo in Guangxi. Yi women in Liangshan are fond of skirts, though some women have taken to wear trousers instead. It is a transition time when both skirts and trousers are fashionable.

That "The back part of the garment is longer than its front" is popular in west Yunnan Province, Chuxiong and southeast Yunnan Province. It is probably the trace of an account in "Literature in Later Han Dynasty" that the national minorities inhabiting in Ailao Mountain area liked to wear "garment with long back hem". The "fire weed cloth" in Chuxiong and other places mirrors the features of human being's collected economy in ancient time.

The main designs in Liangshan and Wumeng Mountain consist of spiral designs and geometrical figures. The style is archaic, plain and bold. Yi people in other regions prefer realistic designs of animals and plants with bright colours. Flames,tiger stripes, sheep horn veins and Eight Diagrams (eight combinations of three whole or broken lines formerly used in divination) are the representative designs. Cockscomb cap, tiger-head cap, musk bag and other ornaments are the symbols of light and justice, luck and happiness, pregnant with the meaning of shunning the evil spirit and avoiding the ghosts, reflecting a strong utilitarianism.

The past and the present of the costumes and adornments of Yi Nationality show us that on the basis of preserving traditions while assimilating cultural factors from other national- ities, Yi costumes are continuously enriching and progressing in pace with the development of society. We can also see the traditional cultural characteristics of Yi people that they like and respect black colour, tiger, fire and force; their traditional concept formed in hundreds of years in the respects of aesthetics, religion, philosophy and customs; and the deepest mentality of Yi people in cultural structure. The traditional costumes of Yi people provide lively historical materials with its rich connotation in history, thought and art to make possible the further understanding of the culture of Yi Nationality.

The Chinese people of all nationalities are engaging in the socialist modern construction. The realization of modernization is a social reform in such respects as economy, politics, culture, lifestyle, and value judgement. In order to fit in with the reform, people's clothing culture will witness significant changes and the traditional costumes and adornments of all nationalities formed in a very long time will be pounded and screened in the mighty torrent of modern civilization. It is our belief that the costumes of Yi Nationality with its great vitality not only had great impact on the prosperous development of Yi people in the past, but also will adapt themselves to the modernized life in the days to come. With their unique national tradition, the costumes of the broad masses of Yi people are sure to have a glorious future.

Our aim in compiling this album is to record and preserve the cultural wealth of the costumes and adornments of Yi Nationality. We hope these lively images will inspire people to understand and feel the great creative power of Yi people and build a bridge which can not be expressed by words between different nationalities with the view of furthering the mutual understanding and friendship between all the nationalities.

September, 1989

全国彝族分布示意图

全国彝族人口简表

项目 省区	分布地区	彝族人口
四川省	凉山彝族自治州	1 336 637 人
	马边彝族自治县	48 711 人
	峨边彝族自治县	27 468 人
	其它各县	112 897 人
	合计	1 525 713 人
云南省	楚雄彝族自治州	570 480 人
	红河哈尼族彝族自治州	724 500 人
	峨山彝族自治县	58 594 人
	宁蒗彝族自治县	95 322 人
	路南彝族自治县	56 488 人
	南涧彝族自治县	80 226 人
	漾濞彝族自治县	30 801 人
	景东彝族自治县	112 826 人
	江城哈尼族彝族自治县	10 941 人
	巍山彝族回族自治县	77 784 人
	寻甸回族彝族自治县	36 074 人
	元江哈尼族彝族傣族自治县	35 466 人
	新平彝族傣族自治县	100 433 人
	禄劝彝族苗族自治县	85 283 人
	普洱哈尼族彝族自治县	29 567 人
	景谷傣族彝族自治县	48 194 人
	其它各县	1 202 014 人
	合计	3 354 993 人
贵州省	威宁彝族回族苗族自治县	73 842 人
	其它各县	489 905 人
	合计	563 747 人
广西壮族自治区	隆林各族自治县	2 616 人
	其它各县	2 060 人
	合计	4 676 人
其它省区		4 435 人
总计		5 453 564 人
备注	人口数为 1982 年普查数	

图 例

▲ 彝族分布区域
◎ 省、自治区人民政府驻地
● 自治州人民政府、地区行政公署驻地
● 自治县人民政府驻地
· 县人民政府驻地
—·— 国界
—·— 省界
—·— 自治州界
〜 河流

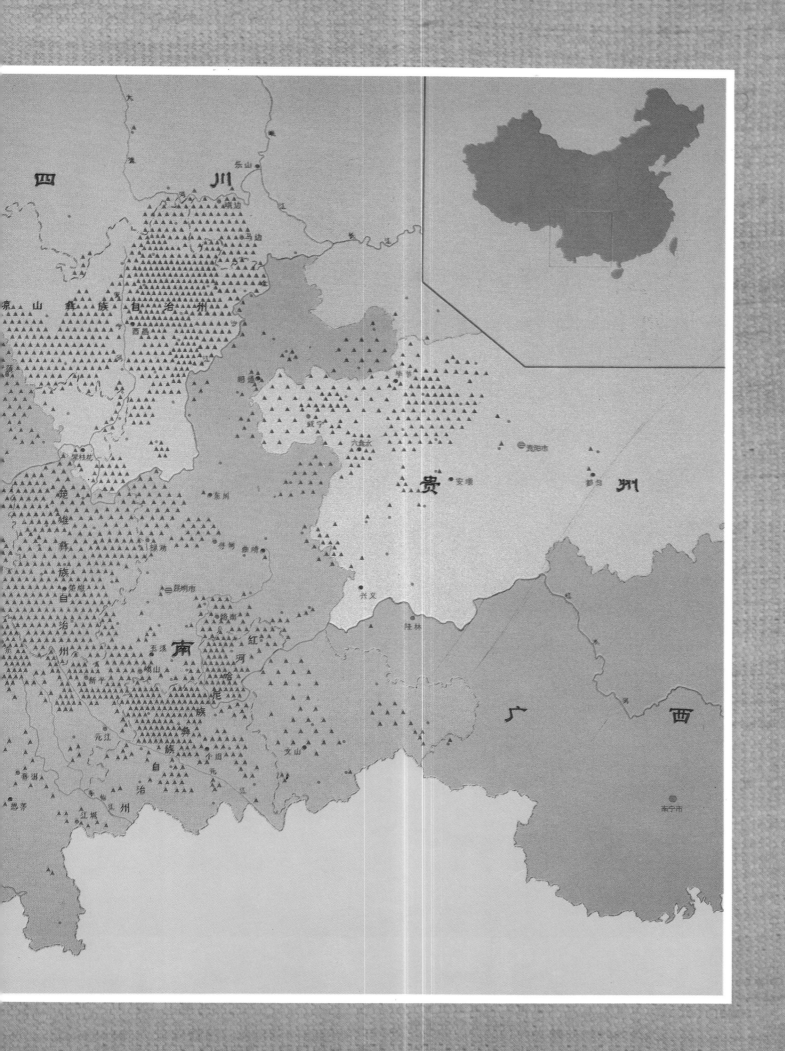

Spinning drawing on bronze shell-keeping utensil unearthed in Shizhai Mountain in Jinning of Yunnan Province (2 BC to late 1 BC).

Hairstyle and garments of Yi women in Daliangshan and Xiaoliangshan are alike to those of the images on the frescoes of the Huo's graveyard (around 385-394) built in East Jin Age which was discovered in Houhaizi of Zhaotong in Yunnan province. Those images with their feet bare. wore felt"Caerwa" and wrapped the headscarf into a "Ziti".

The picture shows the frescoes of the Huo's graveyard and the restored version.

THE LIANGSHAN MODEL

MEIGU STYLE

XIDE STYLE

BUTUO STYLE

Liangshan model of costumes is popular mainly in Liangshan Yi Nationality Autonomous Prefecture and neighbouring counties as well as Jinsha River Region in Yunnan Province. About 1,800,000 people speaking northern dialect of Yi language wear this model of costumes.

High and perilous Daliangshan and Xiaoliangshan are secluded, having little communication with the outside world in the Past. Up to the 1950s, this area still remained in slave society. The style of the garments in this area is unique, plain and archaic, keeping traditional patterns intact. Garments of Yi men at present time are completely alike to those of the images on the frescoes of the Huo's graveyard in Zhaotong of Yunnan Province built in East Jin Age. Those images with their feet bare, wore felt capes and dressed their hair into cone-shaped buns.

In Liangshan, both men and women wear coats which fasten on the right side. People of all ages and both sexes wear "caerwa" (a kind of cape), felt capes, leggings and felt socks. Men are used to preserve a bunch of hair long on the forehead. They wear a headscarf and fold the front part of it into a 20-30 cm cone-shaped knot on one side of the forehead. It is called "hero knot" in common saying. Men wear such ornaments as Mila pearl and silver ring on his left ear. The bottom of the trouser leg is broad, medium-sized or narrow in different regions or according to people speaking different languages. Women wear skirts and headscarfs. After having a baby, they wear hats instead of wrapping their hair with a kerchief. They wear ear ornaments made of gold, silver, coral, jade and sea shells on both ears. They are fond of different neck ornaments, such as silver tablets.

The garments are usually made of black, red and yellow home-woven and home-dyed wool and linen materials. Cross-stitch work, embroidery, lace trimming and other carfts are used to decorate the garments. Steel for flint, sheep horn and spiral designs are traditional patterns. Materials for clothing vary according to wearer's status, taste and age.

Rolling Jinsha River nutures Yi people generation after gneration, creating brilliant culture of Yi nationality.

Gonghai, pearl of Liangshan.

Drinking Gangan wine to one's fill according to tradition.

Joyous torch festival.

MEIGU STYLE

This style of clothing is fashionable in Meigu, Leibo, Ganluo, Mabian and Ebian Counties of Sichuan Province and part in Zhaojue, Jinyang of Sichuan Province and Qiaojia, Yongshan of Yunnan Province. This region is generally known as "broad-legged trousers region". The people who inhabit there speak "Yinuo" dialect. About 400,000 people wear this style of clothing.

The striking characteristic of men's garments is the broad bottoms of the trouser legs.

Women also like to wear wide pleated skirts. The number of pleats sometimes comes to more than one hundred. Girls wear multi-layered headscarfs made of black cloth. Married women increase the layers of their headscarfs. After having a baby, they wear lotus-leaf-shaped bonnets.

Coiled floral design of fine lines is the main pattern in adorning the coats with pasted floral design and embroidery as supporting ones. The caerwa is made of materials in original colour with no tassels on it. It is always edged with broad pieces of black or blue cloth. The style is plain and graceful.

Men are fond of tight-fitting jackets. The prevalent colour are black and blue. Skillful embroidery is usually used to adorn both the sleeves and the front part of the jacket. The remarkable feature is the broad bottoms of the trouser legs, the widest reaching 170 cm.

Floral designs on the sleeves. Embroidery shows exquisite workmanship. Coiled floral designs are the main patterns with cross-stitch work and embroidering as supporting crafts. steel for flint, sheep horn, wave line and spiral designs are often used.

The attire of young men.

Men of Liangshan are fond of different kinds of ornaments. The most unique one is "Tuta", a sash worn over one's shoulder. It is woven with fine tendons of cow. White tablets made of tridacna are inlaid on the sash. In ancient times, "Tuta" was the sash for fastening sabre, so men in Liangshan still cherish this kind of sash and look vigorous and brave when wearing it.

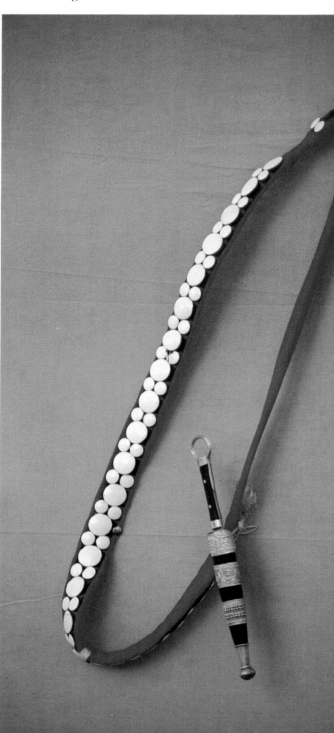

Sabres and silver spice cases for men. The silver spice case is hung by a chain in front of one's chest with moustache clips, earpicks and tobacco picks as pendants. In the view of men in Liangshan, a man is handsome without moustache, so spice cases and moustache clips are indispensable articles to carry along.

Young men when going out carry a square cloth bag on his shoulder to put money, tobacco and other things in it. Embroidery is usually used to adorn the front and the belt of the bag. Middleaged and old men carry a purse made of chamois around the waist to put money and other things in it.

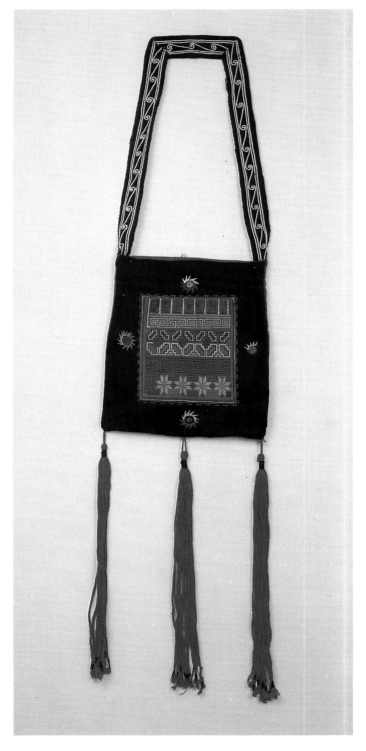

Musk bag made of cloth adorned with long teeth of male river deer on the outside. Yi men in Liangshan like to hang the bag in front of one's chest. It is believed that the musk bag is not only an ornament but also has the function of curing the illness and getting rid of insects.

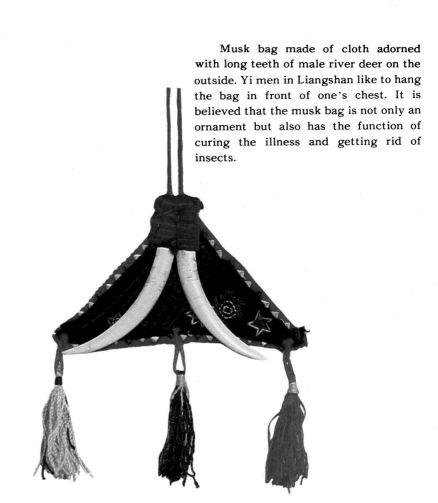

Yi men preserve a bunch of long hair on the forehead. It is called "Zier" in Yi language and "Heaven Buddha" in Han language. It is the sacred and inviolable symbol of men's dignity.(picture 1) . Men wear a headscarf and wrap it into a pointed cone-shaped knot on one side of the forehead which is called "Ziti" in Yi language and "Hero knot"in Han language. The hero knot of young men is as thin as a bamboo shot, 20 -30 cm long (picture 2). Old men wrap their hero knot in a screw bun shape and rest it in the middle of the forehead (picture 3),and some prefer a round bun (picture 4). The method of wrapping headscarf is the same in different areas, that is from right to left. The dead body's knot is from left to right. Yi men all wrap hero knots, but the position is different, some on the right side and some on the left. According to popular legend, when the ancestors of Yi nationality moved from Yunnan and Guizhou Provinces to Liangshan, Qunie clan crossed Jinsha River from the left, while Guhou clan from the right. That is why the descendants of Qunie clan wrap the hero knot on the Ieft side, while the descendants of Guhou clan on the right.

Men in Ganluo drink gangan
wine to their fill.

There is no marked seasonal difference in the costumes of Liangshan style. The people there wear unlined jackets all the year round. But men and women, old and young have to wear felt capes (called "Jieshan" in Yi language) and caerwa (called "wala" in Yi language) to adapt the change of weather. These capes can keep off the wind in the day and be used as quilts at night. Yi people always carry these capes with them. when the wearer is dead, the cape will be burned with the dead body. This is one of the important costumes of Yi people.

White cape, 87 cm long. (upper)

White cape, 87 cm long. (upper)
Caerwa in Meigu area made of more than ten pieces of coarse cloth, most in original colour, no tassels. The edges of front and back parts and the lower hems are all trimmed with black cloth. The sharp contrast between black and white is very appealing to the eye. (lower left)
Caerwa in Xide area. (lower right)

28

They are sewing the caerwa.

Felt socks which men and women wear in the winter. The socks are made from rolling, wool some with bottom and some without bottom. (left) Flax shoes with felt soles. (right)

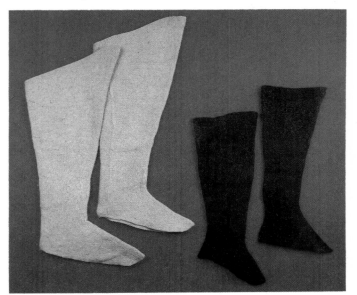

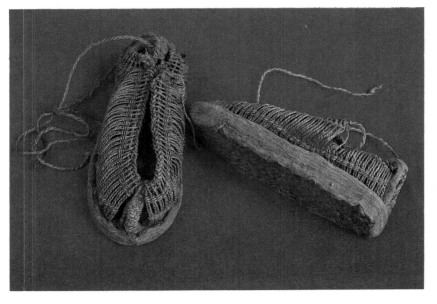

Dress for young women. Old and young women in Liangshan all wear coats with the opening on the right side and long pleated skirts. Skirts for girls are of two-section type. When coming of age, girls hold skirt-changing ceremony and thereafter wear colourful skirts for young women which are of three-section type. The upper section is the skirt waist, the middle section is tube-shaped and the lower section has pleats. The skirt is usually 85 cm long with the number of pleats coming to one hundred and the circumference 200 cm. Young women's skirts of this style are mostly in white and multi-colour. They like to piece red, pink, yellow and green cloth together. The sharp contrast of these colours is remarkable and appealing to the eye. Middle-aged and old women wear long skirts in dull colours.

Traditional women's dress. At present time, brides always wear dress of this style.

Triangular purse with tassels for women. Embroidery is usually used to decorate the front cover. Women wear it on the right side of waist and put needles, thread and tobacco leaves in it. It is an indispensable ornament for women.

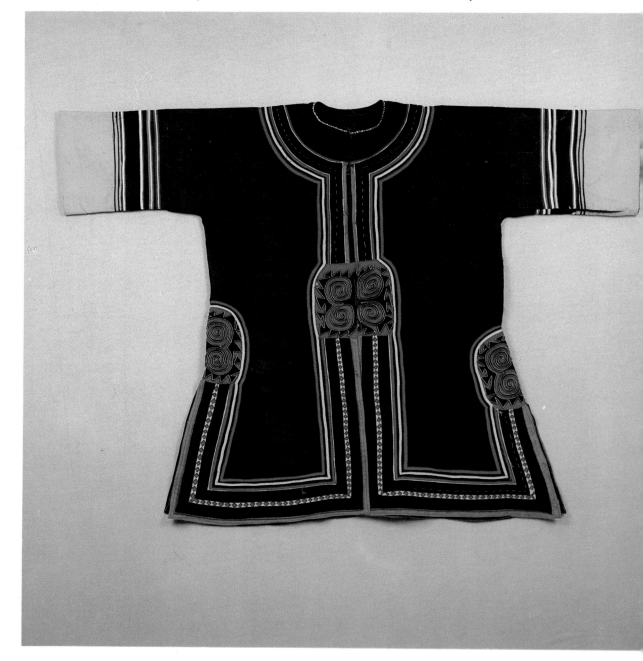

30

Yi women wear shirts, outer coats and sleeveless jackets. Coiled floral design of fine lines is the main pattern for young women, while appliqué and embroidery are also used. Middle-aged women trim the shoulders, hemlines and sleeves with broad black cotton border and decorate red, yellow and green fine line designs on it. Old women wear broad sleeved loose-fitting coats edged with black cloth only.

Young women of Meigu.

Dress for young women in Meigu.

Dress for young women in Zhaotong.

31

In Yi women's view, a woman with long neck is beautiful, so they think highly of neck ornaments. The collar of woman's outer coat is separated from the coat. Silver bulbs and coloured embroidered designs are decorated on the cover of collar. when in full dress, woman wear a rectangular silver tablet on the neck, making a graceful sight.

Collar of the coat.

Dress for middle-aged women in Ebian.

Girl's dress of Mabian.

Hairdress is one of the main signs to distinguish costumes of different dialect areas. In this style, girls wear multi-layered blue cloth kerchief and rest their plaits on it. Married women increase the number of layers. After having a baby, they wear lotus leaf-shaped bonnets. The below is the hairdress of young women.

Lotus leaf-shaped bonnet for middle-aged and old women, the diameter being 44.5 cm.

The back of young people's hairdress.

Flower and grass design is the most typical pattern of the embroidered headscarf of this style.

XIDE STYLE

Costumes of this style are popular in Xide, Yuexi, Mianning Counties of Sichuan Province and part in Xichang, Yanyuan, Muli, Zhaojue, Jinyang, Dechang, Yanbian, Shimian, Jiulong, Luding of Sichuan Province and Ninglang, Zhongdian Counties of Yunnan Province. It is called "medium-size-legged trousers area". About 800,000 people speaking Shengzha dialect wear costumes of this style.

The bottom of trouser leg is 60-100 cm wide. Though it is narrower than Yinuo style broad-legged trousers but still looks like skirt.

Women wear a narrow-sleeved long jacket and match it with a waistcoat. "Cockscomb designs" inlaid with coloured cloth are the main decorative pattern and the colours are harmonious. Young women in Xide, Yuexi and Mianning initiate a fresh style in edging the sleeves and hems of their waistcoats with white rabbit fur. The waistcoat is used as a shoulder pad when the wearer is working. Delicate embroidery makes it one of the costumes with characteristic features. They wear rectangular cross-stitched kerchiefs on the head.

Caerwa is often dyed black or blue, 100 cm long. It is decorated with tassels. The shoulders, edges of front and back parts and hems are trimmed with red, yellow and green teeth-shaped lace or with embroidered continuous floral designs. The style has its distinctive features.

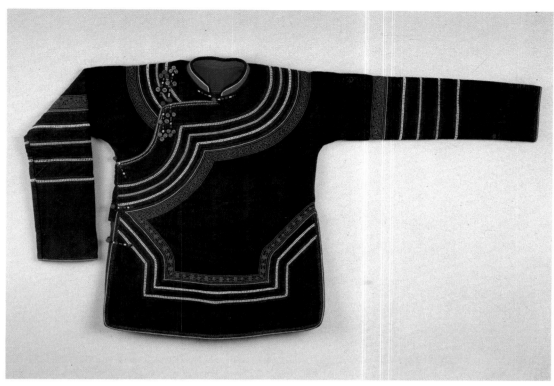

Jackets for young men. The length of the jacket is 80 cm, chest measurement 84 cm, length of sleeve 51 cm and the cuff 9 cm.

Men's garments on the upper part consist of an underwear, an outer coat and a sleeveless jacket. The underwear is usually a white cotton cloth shirt. The outer coat with short collar has the opening on the right side. Black or blue cotton cloth is often used. Young men wear tight-fitting and narrow-sleeved outer garments. The shoulders, front and back parts as well as hems are all edged with several teeth-shaped fine lines made of coloured cloth. Middle-aged and old men like to wear outer coats with buttons down the front or on the right side. The coats have no designs but only long button loops on them.

The sleeveless jacket is skillfully decorated. Middle-aged and young people wear it when going to a village fair or a meeting. It is also used as shoulder pad when the wearer is working.

Sleeveless jacket. The length is 76 cm and chest measurement 100 cm.

Men's hairdress.

In this style, most young men do not wear headscarfs. Middle-aged men like to twist the headscarf into narrow strips and overlap them or arrange them in order and then dress their hair with the headscarf. Men all wear big red or yellow Mila pearls with 15 cm black thread tassels hanging down.

Underwear, outer coats and trousers for old people. The length of trousers is 108 cm, the bottom of trouser leg 60 cm and the waist 65 cm.

37

Young women's narrow-sleeved long jackets of this style.

The waistcoat has black colour as its background. Floral designs are embroidered around the shoulders and on the hemlines of the front part. white rabbit fur embroidered along the edges of the waistcoat's shoulders and lower hems are graceful and elegant. This attire is the unique pattern of this style.

Young women's head-scarf in Mianning area. There is a 40cm long streamer sewn on the back of the headscarf, creating a new style.

Young women's headscarf in Xide area.

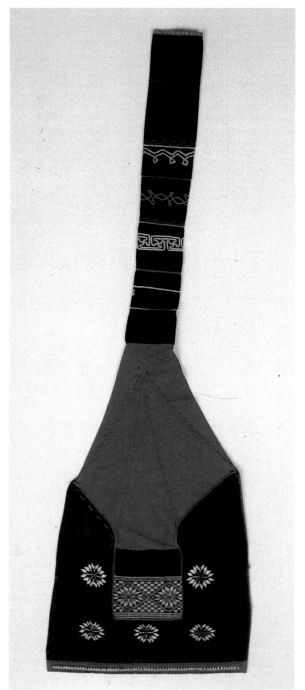

The remarkable feature of this style of costumes is the floral part. The floral design is made of strips of triangular and rhombic borders of this pattern. Floral designs on the jackets of middle-aged the colours are not so rich and there is less designs. This is a dress design inlaid around the shoulders and on the hemlines of the front coloured cloth. Sometimes a dress or headscarf has four or five floral and old women are always the same as those for young women, but for middle-aged woman.

A Yi girl with silver ornaments in her hands (left) and a married woman with head-cover in her hands (right) are dressing up the bride (middle). This attire shows the difference in their age. One can distinguish a married woman from an unmarried woman by the colour of their dress and their headwear.

Head-cover with silver ornaments. Yi women are particular about the head cover for wedding. It is double layered and in round radiation shape. The materials, colours and ornaments are not always the same but are all pregnant with the meaning of joy and happiness.

Attire for middle-aged and old women.

BUTUO STYLE

This style of costumes and adornments is popular in Butuo and Puge Counties in Sichuan Province, part of Jinyang, Ningnan, Huili, Huidong, De'chang, Xichang, Zhaojue, Yanyuan, Miyi Counties of Sichuan Province and Yuanmou, Huaping Counties of Yunnan Province. It is known as "narrow-legged trousers region". About 600,000 people speaking "Suodi" dialect wear this style of costumes and adornments.

The outstanding feature of men's garments of this style is the riding breetches-shaped trousers with small bottoms of trouser legs, wide waist and loose crotches. The jacket is very short, ususally above the navel and with many closely arranged long button loops on it. They wear caerwa skillfully made of goat skin, dress their hair on the crown, wrap a headscarf but do not fold it into a hero knot.

Women are fond of wearing a short-sleeved coat which fastens on the right side over the jacket. The coat is so short as not to reach the navel. Colourful designs are decorated all over the coat. The style is bold, plain, graceful and with classic beauty. The skirt is very thick, often made of woolen. A symbolic small-sleeved felt cape is worn outside the dress. Young women like to wear a black cotton kerchief lockstitched with colourful thread which is wound up in a standing straight shape to rest on the forehead. Women of Yuanmo wear high black tube-shaped hats. After having a baby, they wear a big disc-shaped hat with a round bamboo frame at the top.

Men are fond of short jackets and narrow-legged trousers.

length of jacket 40.8 cm

chest measurement 94.4 cm

length of sleeve 54 cm

cuff 4 cm

length of trousers 93 cm

width of waist 96 cm

bottom of trouser leg 14 cm

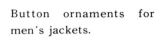
Attire for young men.

Button ornaments for men's jackets.

Men of Butuo area like caerwa made of thick and heavy goat skin. The tailoring method of this kind of caerwa is particular. They have to prepare the skins of five goats of the same age (usually three years old), of the same colour and which are killed at the suitable time, process them by special method and skillfully make them into caerwa. Black fur is considered first-class. Because of the strict requirements of the tailoring method, this kind of caerwa is the treasure of costumes. Men wear it on festivals and ceremonial occasions.

Young women's attire of this style consists of a long gown reaching to the knees, a half-sleeved short coat with buttons on the right side and slits on both sides and a pleated skirt to match them. The coat which is above the naval is wholly decorated with traditional wave lines and spiral designs. Appliqué is the main pattern supported with coiled floral designs and inlaid work. Black, red and yellow are the basic colours. The style is archaic, plain and bold.

Girls of Puge in full dress.

Triangular bags for women.

03 Dress for middle-aged women.

Going to the village fair.

A young girl wearing a wide-brimmed hat made of yak fur felt.

Outer coat, long skirt. The thick skirt is woven of pure wool. There are pleats no the border of the skirt, but no pleats or few pleats on the upper part. A woman looks graceful when wearing it.

Attire for bride and brides-maid.

Designs on the back of a blouse.

Women wearing symbolic small-sleeved felt coats.

Mother and daughter. After having a baby, women wear a round plate shaped hat made of black cloth and with a bamboo frame. They dress their hair into the hat.

A Yi woman of Yuanmou area in Yi Nationality Autonomous prefecture in Chuxiong of Yunnan Province wearing a high tube shaped hat made of black cloth (there is a bamboo hat inside), a short jacket and a long skirt. A triangular purse and a musk bag are hanging on her waistbelt. The mode of costume is different from the women's dress of Butuo model, but the styles are alike.

Young women's dress of Yuanmou.

Wide-brimmed hat made of silver tablets and felt and cape made of horse tails for sacrificial rites. The cape is made of the tails of forty horses. The cape is in black colour and looks bright. It is a rare treasure in Liangshan Region.

48

A colourful painting suit of armour is a protective garment with painted designs. It is made up of a front piece and a back piece. Each piece has a upper part and a lower part. The upper part on the front or the back consists of five pieces of hard skin to protect the chest. Skin strips are used to link up more than 300 pieces of rectangular skin to form the lower part which looks a short skirt to protect the stomach. Coloured painting designs are pregnant with the meaning of preventing spears and avoiding arrows to bless the wearer with safety and victory. (upper right)

Yi knight`s attire.

Cotton-padded war garment with opening on the right side, round-collar, short-sleeved, tight-fitting. The material is pieced together with "pulu" (a woolen fabric made in Xizang) or woolen fabrics lined with a layer of cotton inside and sewn with small stitches. So the garment is fast, thick and heavy enough to resist knives and arrows. (lower right)

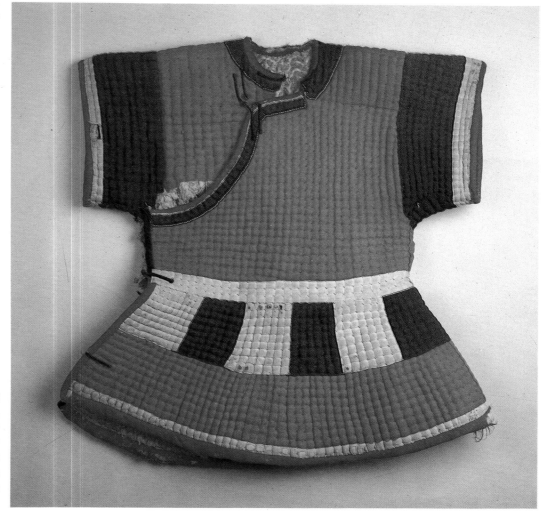

In the opinion of Yi nationality in Liangshan, silver is the symbol of beauty and wealth. People try their best to adorn oneself with all kinds of silver ornaments. These traditional silver ornaments are all handwork of Yi silver-smiths. The silver ornaments are exquisite in workmanship and unique in style.

Gold-plated silver cape for bride of Liangshan.

Traditional gold-plated silver breast ornaments for bride only. It is called "zhezhefu" in Yi language. It weighs about 2,500g.

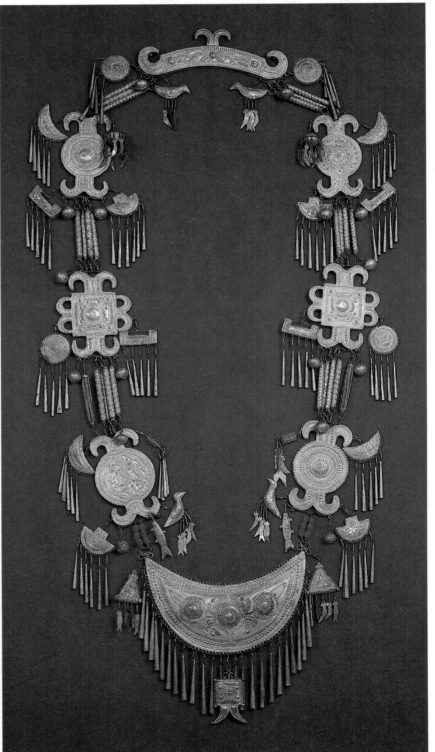

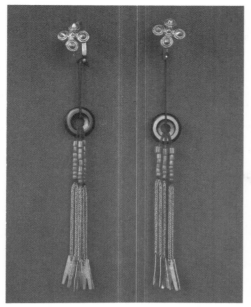

Earpendants of Yongshan
in Yunnan Province.

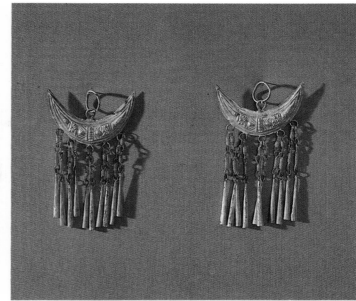

Moon-shaped earrings of Mabian
in Sichuan Province

Women's neck ornaments of
Ninglang of Yunnan Province.

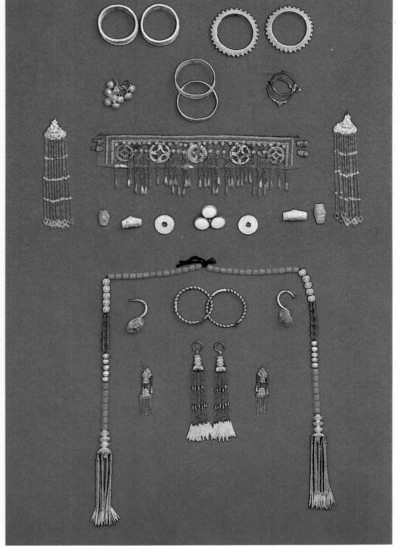

Various kinds of silver
ornament of Liangshan in
Sichuan Province.

THE WUMENG MOUNTAIN MODEL

WEINING STYLE

PANLONG STYLE

This model of costumes and adornments is popular in Bijie Region and Liupanshui City in Guizhou Province; Zhenxiong, Yiliang, Weixin in Zhaotong of Yunnan Province as well as Xuyong, Gulin in Sichuan Province and Longlin in Guangxi More than 900,000 people speaking eastern dialect of Yi language wear this kind of costumes and adornments.

Wumeng Mountain, birthplace of the culture of Yi nationality since ancient times, was the main communication line linking the ancient Central Plains up with southwestern area. In the old days, the costumes and adornments of Yi nationality and those in Liangshan were most alike but with slight difference. Since Ming and Qing Dynasties, there has been much alternation in the styles of costumes.

This model of costumes and adornments used to be made mainly of woolen and linen, but now often made of cotton materials. Yi people like and value black colour, so they prefer materials in black or blue. The basic pattern of this model is a long gown with buttons on the right side and a pair of trousers. The shoulders, collar, hems and skirt borders are all trimmed with floral adornments.

According to the characteristics of different regions, there are Weining style and Panlong style in this model of costumes and adornments.

Imposing Wumeng Mountain.

Pastureland in the mountain.

Picking tea.

Yi nationality villages.

WEINING STYLE

This style of costumes is popular in eight counties in Bijie of Guizhou Province; Liuzhi, Shuicheng in Liupanshui City and Zhenxiong, Yiliang, Weixin in Zhaotong of Yunnan Province as well as Xuyong, Culin in Sichuan Province. About 800,000 people wear this style of costumes.

Men and women always wear black or blue long gowns with buttons on the right side, trousers, black or white headscarfs, waistbands often made of white cloth and embroidered sparrow hawk-shaped shoes with high spikes. Men have no designs on their garments and wear woolen felt capes when going out. The collar, cuffs, hems and bottoms of trouser legs of women's dress are trimmed with colourful complex designs. This style of costumes is called in Han language reverse shoulder pad, broad embroidered border and four hanging pillars (The four long floral design borders on the front, back, left and right slits of the long gown are like four hanging pillars). Women wear ʌ-shaped black scarfs with a band tightened on the fore-head (it is called "Lezi"). They wear such silver ornaments as earrirgs, bracelets and rings. Married women wear eardrops instead of earrings, white or embroidered short aprons and floral streamers on their back.

Men's garments of this style consist of a black headscarf, a long gown with buttons on the right side, a pair of trousers, a waistband, a pair of sparrow haw- kshaped shoes with high spike and a woolen felt cape when the weather is cold.

Men's jacket made of pure wool with buttons down the front.

This is a popular garment for men in pastoral area.

Woolen felt cape.

Shoulder bag.

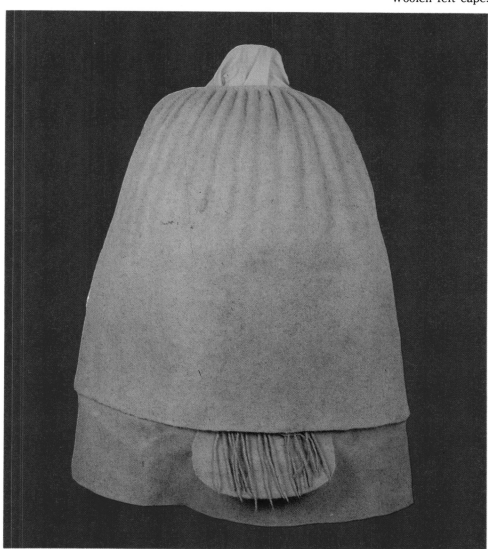

Sandals with spiral designs. (below).

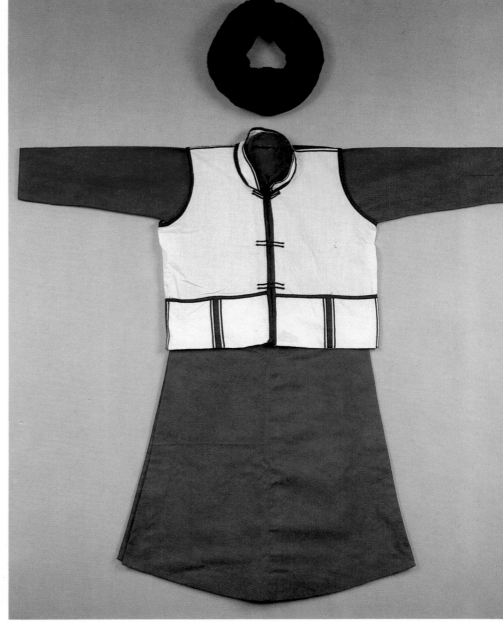

Men and women of Yi nationality in Wumeng Mountain always wear jackets with many pockets (It is called "white cloth tata" in common saying) over the long gown when working. The jacke are usually made of white cloth with some designs on the hem.Some jackets have buttons down the front and some jackets' back part is longer than the front part. The right is boys' wear. The below is white cloth tata for adults.

Yi people like to drink roasted tea which is fragrant, rich in flavour and a little bitter.

Middle-aged and young men of Weining and Hezhang dressed their hair into a round bun and wrapped it with black kerchief in the past. They wear jackets with the opening down the front and broad-legged trousers. The embroidered trouser belt is always the token given by his lover.

A Yi man is hunting.

Yi men's sleeveless jacket with buttons down the front in Qing Dynasty.

The attire of Yi women in northwest Guizhou Province and northeast Yunnan province consists of a ∧-shaped black headscarf covered with a square embroidered kerchief, an embroidered long gown with buttons on the right side, a pair of embroidered trousers, a white waistband and an apron trimmed with lace, a pair of cloth socks and a pair of sparrow hawk-shaped shoes as well as earings, bracelets, rings and other silver ornaments.

Broad-legged trousers with cross-stitched designs.

Women's long gown and apron.

Cloth socks and embroided shoes.

Apron for women.

Designs for women's blouse.

The complex floral linear design around the collar is called "Bilituoluo" in Yi language, meaning a "round universe", and "shoulder pad in opposite direction" in Han language, meaning all things in the universe. Floral linear designs are embroidered on the edges of the four slits. They look like four hanging pillars, so they are called "four hanging pillars" in Han language. On the lower hem, there are three spiral designs in the shape of a tiger head. The designs are made by coiling white cloth strips or fine threads. The white spiral design is called "Mupumugulu" in Yi language, meaning "Heaven father", while the black spiral design on the background is called "Mimomian" in Yi language, meaning "Ground mother". The designs are the symbols of Yi nationality's ancient philosophic thoughts about the positive and negative principles in nature, the Five Elements (metal, wood, water, fire and earth to which the ancient Chinese scholars attributed the origin of the physical world) and the Eight Diagrams (eight combinations of three whole or broken lines formerly used in divination) and tiger world outlook.

Women's long gown of Nayong County. The main pattern is appliqué in bold style.

Tiger head-shaped face guard was worn by Yi bride in Bijie before liberation to prevent people from seeing the face of the bride. As a result of textual research, this custom has its origin in Yi ancestors' totem--female tiger.

Yi bride's attire of Bijie. She wears a black silk headscarf covered with an embroidered kerchief, a silver "lezi" (a kind of band) on the forehead, a tiger head-shaped face guard, a long gown with "four hanging pillars", a pair of trousers, a waistcoat with black flowers on red background worn over the gown, a shawl made of strings of pearls, a floral waist band and a pair of embroidered shoes.

Yi bride's wedding gown in Hezhang at the end of Qing Dynasty.

Yi women's long gown and waistcoat in Nayong at the end of Qing Dynasty.

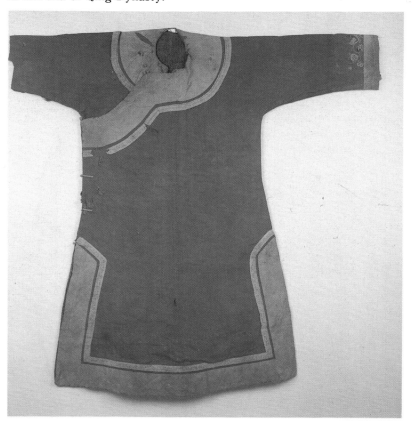

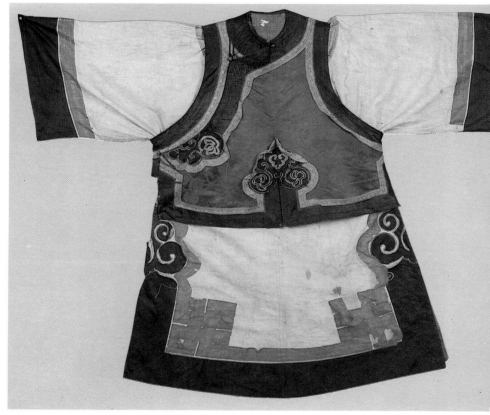

Patterns of children's wear. Boy's and girls all wear long gowns and trousers. Boy's wear has no designs. The designs on girl's wear are the same as those on women's gowns. The inlaid work and embroidered designs of taiji, tiger head, Eight Diagrams, flowers, birds and butterfies on children's hats, abdomen cover and fans are delicate and elegant.

Bijie Girl

Girl's bonnets. The designs and the spice bags with anima designs imply the meaning of shunning evil spirit and avoid the ghost.

Styles, patterns and hairdress of Yi women in Majie, Weining of Guizhou Province have the characteristics of both Liangshan style and Wumeng Mountain style. Their hair is wrapped with black cloth in the shape of a dish. They overlap long floral bands on their forehead, with silver"lezi" as decoration. They wear floral gowns with opening on the right side, long pleated skirt with several parts, white waistband and embroidered shoes.

Women's costumes and adornments

Floral bands as hairdress

Young girls

65

Cape. This cape is the mourning apparel for the eldest daughter-in-law of the dead. Yi people of Panxian County have this custom.

The garments for the Master in memorial ceremony of Yi people in Zhaotong. The attire consists of a "Lehei" (a black band with pendants) on the forehead, a long gown, "Moqi" (a kind of talisman) in two hands, a fairy tube on the shoulder, fairy eardrops on both ears and such instruments used in a religious ceremony as Eight Diagrams, scriptures and eighteen charts to pay tribute to the memory of their ancestors or to show the way for the dead.

The official garment for An's chief headman of Yi people in Dapo Village, Kele District of He-zhang County.

Square gown."Dading County History" of Qing Dynasty reported, Yi women in
Shuixi Region wore square gowns. They took small pieces of coloured cloth,
embroidered flowers, birds and animals on them and sewed the pieces into a
square material, 67 cm each. A square gown was made with dozens of these
materials. The front part of the gown was longer than the back part. Both front and
back parts were sewed together with an opening on the top. Yi women wore the
gown by pulling it over the head. The gown had lining in it. Poor people used cloth
as lining, while the rich used   silk . They wore the gown over other garments.
Brides wore this gown in the first three days after the wedding to entertain
visitors, but not wear it at ordinary times. This square gown is the wedding gown
of the wife of An's chief headman of Yi penple in Dapo Village, Kele District of
Hezhang county.The gown is 240 cm long and 240 cm wide. It was reported that
the gown was embroidered by the bride's slave girl who came from her parent's
home.

The gown is kept in the Museum of Guizhou Province.

Design of the right front part of the square gown.

Design of the left front part of the square gown.

Design of the back part of the square gown.

69

The riding dress for the wife of An`s chief headman of Yi people in Dapo Village, Kele District of Hezhang County.

Cross-stitch work is one of the crafts which are popular among Yi women of Wumeng Mountain.

The gown is 65.5 cm long and the sleeve is 119 cm long.

The main patterns of Weining style are tigers, spiders, cuckoos, azaleas and other animal or plant designs as well as spiral and octagon designs. The typical one is spiral design. Cross-stitch work, embroidery and inlaid work are usually used to decorate the dress.

Cross-stitched designs on the brims of bed-curtain.

Headscarf for covering the head used by Yi girls at wedding. The designs are beautiful, cross-stitched

Lockstitching and embroidering designs of flowers and birds in the middle of suspenders.

Inlaid and embroidering designs in the middle of suspenders.

Inlaid work and appliqué designs in the middle of suspenders.

Designs on the back apron.

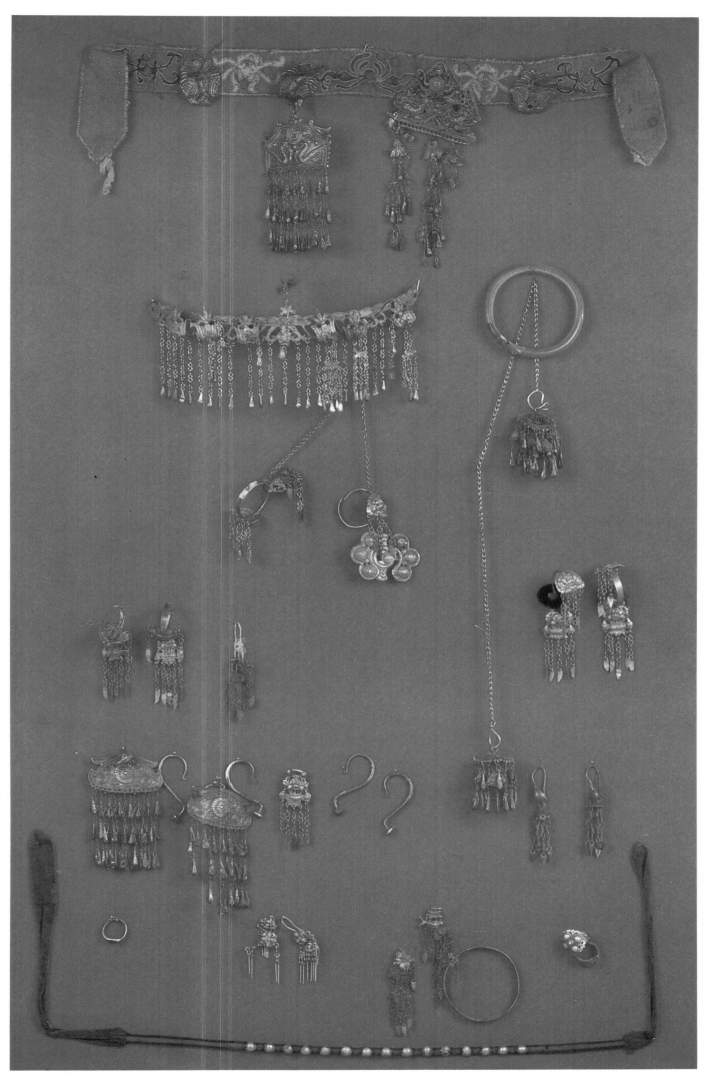

Silver ornaments (forehead bands, eardrops, bracelets and rings).

PANLONG STYLE

This style of costumes and adornments is fashionable from the south of Panxian County in Guizhou Province to Longlin in Guangxi. About 100,000 people wear this style of costumes and adornments.

Men and women's main garment of this style is a long gown in black or blue with buttons on the right side. This style and Weining style are largely identical but with minor differences. The headscarfs are usually in white colour. There are less designs on women's dress. The waist is girded with a black apron with two floral streamers hanging down on the front. women of Longlin wear a blouse with buttons on the right side. Embroidery is used to adorn the hemlines. The waist is girded with a black short apron. They wear trousers in dark colours or wide and long skirts. They only adorn a few floral designs on the slits of the garments or borders of the skirts. Women's dress of Longlin style look more plain and graceful than Yi women's garments of Weining style. They also wear black headscarfs, earrings, bracelets and embroidered shoes with a hawk head on the top.

Men's garments are mainly the same as Weining style. They wear a long gown with opening on the right side, a pair of trousers, all in black and blue colours, a headscarf, a waist-band, but no goat skin cape. In the picture is men's garments of Longlin.

Yi women in Panxian County.

Women's long gowns and trousers of Panxian County.

Women's hereditary blouse of Panxian County.

The blouse of this pattern is the hereditary dress for the eldest daughter-in-law of "Zumo" (the head of a clan) of Yi people in Panxian County. The blouse has a collar but no opening in the front. The sleeves are not sewn together. Three lines of hexagon designs are embroidered on both the left and the right shoulder. This is an ancient dress of Yi people. It is the symbol of feudal patriarchal system of the right of primogeniture in Panxian County. In Dafang, this is the ceremonial robe for bride, who wears it over the long gown to entertain guests during three days after the wedding.

Yi women' shirts.

Yi women in Longlin of Guangxi now like to wear a blouse with buttons on the right side and edged with lace.

The waist is girded with a black short apron. They wear trousers in dark colours and embroidered shoes. There are a few designs on the slits of the gown and the border of the skirt. The dresses of this style are more plain and graceful than those of Weining style. In the picture, it is a suit of traditional blouse and skirt.

Suspender in Longlin. Appliqué and embroidery are used for decoration. The main designs are flowers and birds. The colours are rich and gorgeous.

THE HONGHE MODEL

YUANYANG STYLE

JIANSHUI STYLE

SHIPING STYLE

This style of costumes and adornments is popular in the southern area of Yunnan Province inhabited by Yi people, up to Kaiyuan, Mengzi in the east, Jinping, Jiangcheng in the south, Puer, Shuangbai in the west and Kunming in the north. Honghe River flows into this area along the vast Ailao Mountain. Various reasons concerning history, goegraphy and nationalities account for the unbalance of the political, economic and cultural development as well as the rich and colourful costumes and adornments in the southern area of Yunnan Province inhabited by Yi people.

About 900,000 people wear this style of costumes and adornment. Most of them speak southern dialect of Yi language.

Men's garments are almost the same in different places. They always wear an upright-collared jacket with buttons down the front and a pair of trousers with loose crotch.

Honghe River flowing into the south of Yunnan Province along Ailao Mountain nutures Yi penple who inhabit here generation after generation.

High moutains and terraced fields make the south of Honghe River a prosperous and beautiful place.

Yi people wearing garments of this style always build their villages at the foot of a mountain or near the fields. The houses are mainly made of earth, called "Tuzhangfang". Recently there are more tile-roofed houses.

Yi girls in full dress in the festivals.

YUANYANG STYLE

This style of costumes and adornments is popular in mountain areas in Yuanyang, Xinping, Honghe, Jinping, Luchun, Jiangcheng and Mojiang Counties.

This style has its distinctive feature in women's wear. They like blue, green, red and yellow coloured cloth for material and decorate their dress with silver bulbs and silver chains, making a pleasant and attractive sight.

A blouse which has buttons on the right side and high slits is the main dress for women. They always wear a long-sleeved blouse (or a blouse with oversleeves) with floral designs and on the outside of the blouse, a half-sleeved coat reaching to the knees or shanks. Women in Yuanyang and Jinping are fond of sleevesless jackets. They wear broad-legged trousers and gird the waist with a waistbelt. Sometimes they have the habit of pulling the front part of the coat to one's back.

The shoulders, borders of the front part, sleeves and lower hems of the coat are often decorated with designs, but there are less designs on the trousers. Appliqué is the main craft while embroidery and inlaid work are also used. Geometrical lines are used as the main features of the designs.

Hairdress: Girls like to wear a cockscomb cap inlaid with silver bulbs. Some wrap their hair into a headscarf. Married women always wear wrappers.

Girls wearing caps with silver bulbs are the outstanding characteristic of womes's wear of this style. Silver caps are fashionable in Honghe, Yuanyang, Luchun and Jinping. The cap which is called "cockscomb cap" because its shape is just like a cockscomb has its origin in the legend that the cock can subdue the demons and tame the ghosts. It is the symbol of luck and happiness for Yi girls. The big and small bulbs on the cap symbolizing stars and the moon imply that the light always accompanies the girls. In the upper picture is a girl in Jinping wearing a high silver cap.

Young women's long gown and sleeveless jacket inlaid with silver bulbs of Yuanyang.

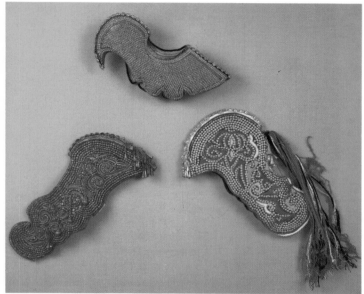

Silver cap in Honghe (middle) and Yuanyang (left, right).

Women's wear include underwear, outer coat, trousers, hat (kerchief), waistbelt and adornments.

The underwear is a coat with long and narrow sleeves and with buttons on the right side. Embroidered designs of flower, bird, insect, butterfly as well as silver bulb and geometrical design are embroidered on it. Young women like to use white cloth for the background of embroidery while old women like black cloth. Outside the coat, there is a half-sleeved blouse reaching beneath the knee with opening on the right side. They pull the back part of the coat to the back of the knee and girded it with a waistbelt, lift the front part to the left and insert it in the waistbelt to expose the smaller and inner piece of the coat which is trimmed with lace. Young women always wear sleeveless jackets inlaid with silver bulbs during the festivals in the winter and on wedding and funeral occasions.

Women like to wear broad-legged trousers trimmed with two lines of blue cloth with no difference in ages. Broad waistbelts with silver bulbs are the outstanding adornment in women's wear of Yuanyang County with the two broad endings hanging down from the back of the waist, making a unique sight.

The silver hat worn by girls has coloured cloth as background and is inlaid with silver bulbs. Girls wear a band inlaid with silver bulbs on the forehead to match the hat, Married women wear kerchiefs. But girls inhabiting near the county town have taken to wear cross-stitched black kerchiefs instead of silver caps.

Women's underwear and
trousers in Yuanyang.

Women in Yuanyang skill-
fully expose the inner and
smaller piece of their coat
which has exquisite embroidery on it.

Broad waistbelt is the important adornment of women's
wear of Yuanyang. It is very appealing to the eye.

The traditional silver bulb inlaid work on the end of women's waistbelt of Yuanyang.

In the late 1970s, the new craft of embroidery with white cashmere is fashionable in Yuanyang to replace the silver inlaid work. Embroidered work is light, cheap, easy to wash, while still keeps the traditional splendid style, so it is a favorite of women. Embroidery is used to decorate cuffs and waistbelts. Young women's waistbelts are in beautiful colours, Mile old women have white adornments on their waistbelts. The left is an embroidered waistbelt of young women. The right is the embroidered designs on the cuffs of women's underwear.

Women of Yuanyang like silver ornaments so much that they often buy various kinds of them whatever the cost is. The lower middle is a sleeveless jacket inlaid with silver bulbs. It was the wedding dress for brides sixty or seventy years ago. The right is a silver shawl which brides wore at wedding in the past time. The lower left is a sleeveless jacket for young women, and the lower right is the silver ornaments girded on the waist.

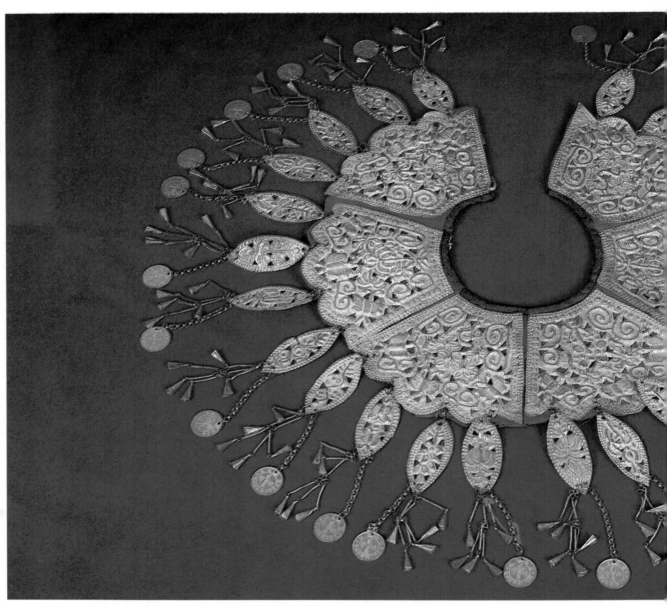

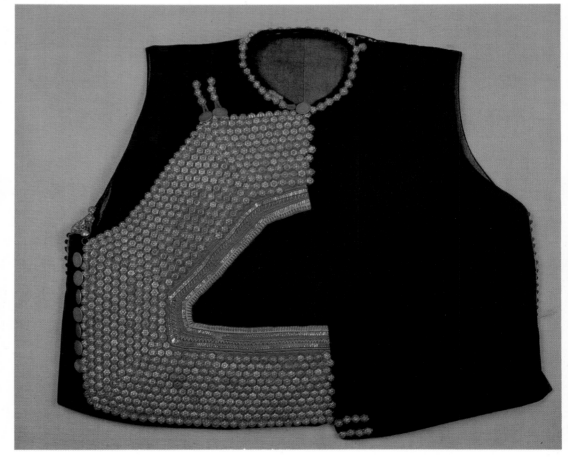

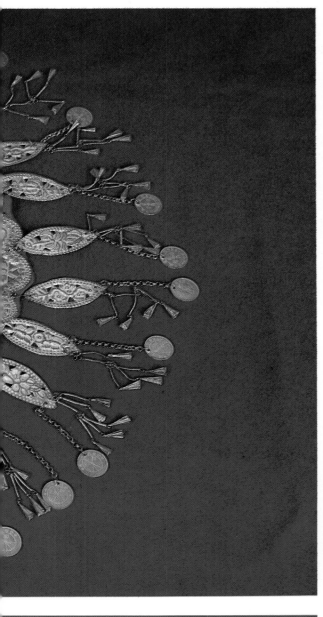

The paper-cut stalls in the streets of Yuanyang are attracting many Yi girls who can do needlework very skillfully. The paper patterns for embroidery are cut by Yi women who work them out in their mind.

Men's wear in Honghe County consists of a upright-collared Jacket with buttons down the front and a pair of trousers with loose crotch. This is the most common pattern of this style.

Women's wear in Honghe County bears some similarities to that in Yuanyang, but its outer coat is shorter than Yuanyang's. Women in Honghe sew two pieces of cloth in different colours together to make their coats. The favorite colours for young women are reddish purple, pale pinkish purple, green and sky blue. The sleeves of the underwear are linked to the over-sleeves. which are decorated with padded floral designs. The trousers are trimmed with laces or bands. The designs vary with ages. The waistbelt with a flat head is a little smaller than that in Yuanyang. It is pieced together with two kinds of coloured cloth.The silver cap worn by girls in Honghe is lower than that in Yuanyang and is inlaid with silver bulbs while silver caps in Yuanyang and jinping are decorated with floral designs. Married women wear kerchiefs. Embroidered shoes are worn when the wearer is in full dress.

Designs of butterflies, flowers and birds are often embroidered on the end of women's waistbelt and waist ornaments. The designs are pregnant with sentiments. It is made by combining the art of embroidering and applique, which are exquisite in workmanship.

Silver collar, blouse and trousers for women in Honghe.

Women's shoes of Honghe.

Yi people's habit of wearing clogs is documented in historical books in Ming and Qing dynasties. Before the 1960s, men in Honghe always wear wooden clogs. At present time, middle-aged and old people still like to wear clogs but change to shoes when going out.

The baby-suspender is not only for practical use but also a work of art. The chief colour tone is red, blue and black which are harmonious with the adornments all over the body. It looks plain, archaic and grave. Most of the designs are dragons, phoenix, flowers and butterflies, implying the bless of mother.

The waistbelts show the unique taste of women in Honghe.

Yi women's attire in Mopan Mountain and Lukui Mountain in Xinping bears simiarities with that of Yuanyang County, with difference in method of decoration and style. Women wear a blue or green blouse and a pair of black trousers with loose crotch. Small floral tablets are decorated on the stomach part of the trousers. The waist is girded with a waistbelt, a band and an embroidered short apron. Both unmarried and married women wrap their hair in a headscarf and wear embroidered shoes. There are two kinds of headscarfs. One kind of headscarfs have the two embroidered endings holding out just like the two wings of a flying bird. The other is a long triangular kerchief with a hard headband on the forehead to match it.

The abdomen ornament of women in Xinping (upper) is in fact the degenerated form of apron, 27 cm wide and 14 cm long. Girdle (middle), waistbelt (lower left), waistband (lower right).

Yi women in Mopan Mountain and Lukui Mountain in Xinping pull the front part of their gown to the back and tie it into a knot to expose the border adornment on the inner piece of the coat. The knot forms a pocket to carry small things.

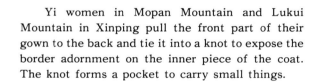

Old women's wear in Daxi Mountain of Eshan County is plain and unadormed.

Yi women of Jiangcheng wear a blue long gown with the front part pulled behind and girded into the waistbelt. Outside the gown, there is a pipa-shaped sleeveless jacket. (pipa is a popular Chinese musical instrument, somewhat shaped like a violin). Girls gird red waistbelts and change to black ones after marriage.

Some Yi women inhabiting on the common border between Lüchun and Honghe wear a black long gown with red sleeves, a pair of black trousers with loose crotch and a hat with silver bulbs. They like to pull the front part of the gown to the back, overlap it and tie a knot beneath the waist. Inlaid designs of dragon, phoenix, peony, fish, butterfly, bird and rattan are used to decorate the shoulders and sleeves of the long gown.

The phoenix design on the back of women's dress.

The style of the sleeves of women's gown
and the designs on it

JIANSHUI STYLE

This style of costumes is popular in the half mountain area, dam area and part of the mountain area in Jianshui, Shiping, Xinping, Eshan, Mengzi, Gejiu, Kaiyuan, Tonghai, Jiangshuan, Yuxi, Yimen, Shuangbai, and Yuanjiang Counties. It is the most common style in this model.

The areas where inhabit Yi people wearing this style of costumes are developed in political, economic and cultural respects. Yi people have an intimate association with Han people, so their costumes and adornments bear some similarities with those of Han people.

Men's wear has its unique style in closely arranged long button loops or silver coin buttons.

Women's attire consists of a coat with buttons on the right side, a pair of broad-legged trousers and a sleeveless jacket or an apron or both outside the gown. There are two kinds of coats: loose-fitting and tight-fitting. The tight-fitting coat is matched with a short apron. Various kinds of techniques are used to decorate the apron in the middle of which is a rhomb-shaped or fan-shaped design. The loose-fitting coat is not matched with any sleeveless jacket. Embroidery is used to decorate the coat, trousers and apron. The colour is dark and graceful. In recent years, tight-fitting coats have replaced loose-fitting ones and become fashionable.

Women's hairdresses vary with different places. Main adornments are silver waist chains and eardrops.

As the saying goes: "white shirt inside and blue jacket outside". This is the characteristic colour and style of tight-fitting women's wear of this style. The traditional women's attire consists of a coat in light colour with buttons on the right side, a sleeveless jacket in dark colour with buttons down the front or on the right side to cover it, a short apron and a pair of blue embroidered trousers. When they wear a sleeveless jacket with silver coin buttons down the front, they usually do not wear any apron.

The picture shows the women's wear in Guanting Village of Gaoshan Mountain area in Jianshui County: coat, trousers (upper), apron (middle right), sleeveless jacket (lower right).

Young women have taken to wear shirts and trousers. instead of coats with buttons on the right side and trousers with loose crotch. But the traditional floral apron is still a favorite of women. The picture shows the girls going to "Kaixin Street" of Eshan on a festive occasion.

Some Yi women of Eshan, Xinping, Shuangbai and Yimen wear loose-fitting coats. Old women's attire still keeps the characteristics of late Qing Dynasty. The picture shows women's coats, trousers and aprons. The arts of trimming, appliqué and cross-stitch work are used to decorate the dress all over the body. The attire is dark in colour and archaic and plain in style.

Women's wear of this style is simple and there are few regional differences. But the hairdress has a unique style. Women in Jianshui tie their plaits with red floss three or four rounds and cover them with a black kerchief. It is called "Three red lines"

Women inhabiting on the common border between Eshan and Shuangbai like to wear trousers with padded, embroidered and painted designs. To decorate the dress with paintings is the style of ancient flower-paintings. The picture shows the designs on the bottoms of women's trousers.

Women's hairdress in Mengzi is to wrap their hair with a towel or a headscarf and dress it into a shape of water caltrop.

Women's headscarf in Laochang Village of Gejiu.

Girls in Anlongbao of Shuangbai like to wear a hat of ancient style called "lezi".

Men's garments of this style consist of a coat with a high upright collar and with buttons down the front, an underwear in light colour and an outer jacket in black or blue. There are designs on the pockets and lower hems. The centipede-shaped button loops on the front part of the coat are only adornments. They can not be buttoned up.

SHIPING STYLE

This style of costumes and adornments is popular in mountain areas in Shiping, Eshan, Mengzi, Kaiyuan, Gejiu, Yanshan, Pingbian, Jinping, Yuanyang and Honghe Counties.

Men's garments are an upright-collared coat with buttons down the front and a pair of broad-legged trousers.

Women's attire consists of a coat with buttons on the right side, a pair of broad-legged trousers and a sleeveless jacket with buttons down the front outside the coat. The hairdress includes kerchiefs, hats, floss, silver bulbs or silver coins.

A narrow-sleeved coat and a sleeveless jacket without buttons are the remarkable characteristics of women's wear. They have the habit of pulling the front part of their coat to the back and wrap it behind the waist. Their coat and trousers are made by piecing together more than two kinds of coloured cloth in sharp contrast. The chief colour tone is red alternating with black. Green, blue and white colours are also used, making a sight appealing to the eye. Various crafts are used to decorate the sleeves, back hem of the coat, borders of the sleeveless jacket, back of the coat and bottoms of trouser legs, with lace-trimming as the main pattern. Flat embroidery is often used in Shiping and Eshan. Besides that, cross-stitching and silver bulb inlaid work are most fashionable in this style. There are remarkable regional differences in designs and patterns.

Women like to wear such silver ornaments as big earrings.

The festive garments of young men in Shiping are often the tokens of promise from the girls they love.

The festive garments of young men in Shiping: jacket, waistbelt, leggings and sandals.

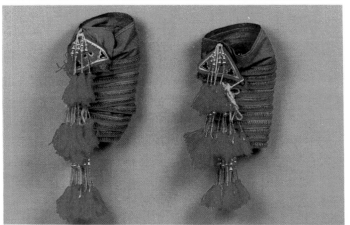

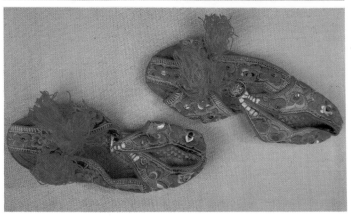

Yi girls living in the neighborhood of Shiping and Eshan like to wear beautiful dresses. Embroidery is used to decorate the clothing all over the body, except trousers. The festive attire of young women consists of more than ten pieces: a headscarf, a long gown, a sleeveless jacket, a silver collar, an undergarment covering the abdomen, a pair of trousers, a waistbelt, a girdle and various kinds of waist ornaments. The picture shows the young men and women going out of the village.

Women's coat of Shiping. There are border ornaments on the inside piece of the coat. They overturn the front part of the coat and pull it to the back of the waist to expose the border ornaments.

Women's headscarf of Shiping, 80 cm long and coil the tassels on the two sides to make a bonnet.

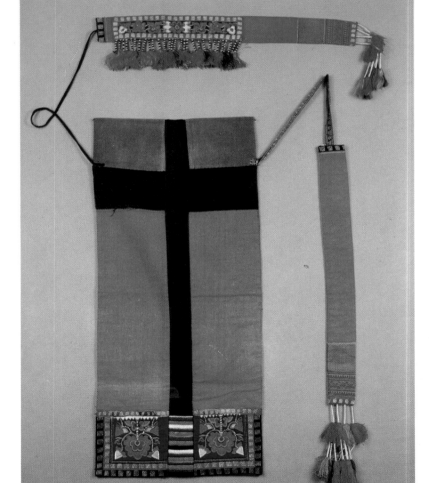

Women's sleeveless jackets of Shiping. There are vertical border ornaments on the front and back parts. Embroidered floral designs or inlaid stripes of coloured cloth (called "Rainbow" in that place) are used to decorate the back of the sleeveless jacket. There is patched floral work of "Sun Flowers" around the collar. Girls have silver "Huobomu (meaning the moon) and "Anudou" (meaning the brassiere) on the chest of the sleeveless jacket.

Women wear a headscarf when working or playing. They wear it all the time except going to bed.

Women in Shiping and Eshan are particular about their waistbelts. They match the waistbelt with their headdress and floral designs on the hems. making the sight more beautiful. The waistbelt is more than 3 meters long.

Young women's waistbelt and waist ornaments of Shiping.

Silk flower designs are always used to decorate women's dress in Shiping and Eshan. The picture shows the silk flower design on the baby-suspender.

Flame designs are inlaid on the back hems, shoulders, cuffs of women's long gowns in Shiping and Eshan. It has origin in the worship of fire by ancient Yi people. The picture shows the design on the back hem.

Women's attire in mountain area in Kaiyuan, Mengzi and Yanshan consists of : a coat, a sleeveless jacket, an apron and a pair of broad-legged trousers. The front and back parts of the trousers are pieced together with cloth of two colours in sharp contrast. Cross-stitching is often used. Hairdress varies according to locality. Some women like to wear a high hat inlaid with silver bulbs, some like a high hat inlaid with silver bulbs and covered with a kerchief and some use artificial hair to dress a big bun. Costumes and adornments are also different to match the hairdress.

Some of the men's garments in the mountain area of Kaiyuan where the mountain is high and the weather is cold still keep the ancient styles: a black jacket with overlapped collar and with an oblique opening in the front and a pair of broad-legged trousers. The borders of the festive coat are trimmed with lace. The waist is girded with a floral apron and a floral waistbelt.

Hairdress for big buns in Beige Village of Kaiyuan was the dowry for brides in the past. After 1950s, brides wear towel kerchiefs to replace this kind of hairdress.

Women's coat and two-coloured trousers in Beige Village of Kaiyuan.

Old women in Mengzi cover a big kerchief on the beautiful hair-dress. It implies that the youth has passed and they have become experienced and prudent.

Women inhabiting on the common border of Jinping and Yuanyang wear black coats and trousers. The cuffs are trimmed with coloured cloth. There are a few designs on the borders of the coat and the bottoms of the trouser legs. They wear a band inlaid with silver bulbs on the forehead and a big black headscarf. The attire of the whole body is simple and refined with the silver bulbs as the only adornment. Silver bulbs are often inlaid on the borders of the sleeveless jacket and the band on the forehead. Young women like pearls and tassels which make them gorgeous in appearance.

THE SOUTHEAST YUNNAN MODEL

LUNAN STYLE

MILE STYLE

WENXI STYLE

This model of costumes is popular in the southeast area of Yunnan Province up to Guangnan, Funing in the east; Maguan, Malipo in the south; Mile, Kaiyuan in the west; Shizong, Kunming in the north; and Napo County of Guangxi Zhuang Autonomous Region as well. A population of 250,000 speaking southeastern dialect of Yi language wear this model of costumes.

The main patterns of women's dress are: a jacket with buttons on the right side, or buttons down the front, and a pair of trousers. In certain areas, women wear skirts. The main patterns of men's clothing are: a jacket with buttons down the front with a sleeveless jacket worn over it, and a pair of trousers with a loose crotch. Some Yi women in Napo of Guangxi and Malipo of Yunnan Province still keep the habit of wearing a kind of ancient pulled-over long robe on festivals and ceremonial occasions.

This model of costumes uses white, blue or black as background with designs of animals and plants or geometric patterns. The crafts include embroidery, inlaid work and batik.

There are three styles of this model of costumes: Lunan, Mile and Wenxi.

Yi nationality's
village in Mile.

Yi nationality in
Malipo celebrating
"Qiaocai" festival.

Moon dance by Yi nationality.

Yi girls from Kunming suburb.

LUNAN STYLE

This style is mainly popular in Lunan, Mile, Qiubei and Kunming of Yunnan Province.

The men's clothing is made of cotton. It is also made of traditional "fire weed" and linen. It is a jacket with buttons down the front worn over with a sleeveless jacket and a pair of trousers with loose crotch.

The women's wear includes a jacket with the back longer than the front and with the buttons on the right side, a pair of medium-length trousers, a skirt, and a decorated cape. The clothes are usually in white and light blue. Girls in Mile like to wear a jacket made with big pieces of black and white materials.

Embroidery is the main craft of this style.

The women's headdress differs from place to place. Women of Guishan, Lunan wear cloth hoop, young girls in Kunming wear cockscomb cap, and young girls twine their two plaits around the head wrapped with a black scarf. The adornment is simple and yet exquisite.

Young men's jacket made of "fire weed cloth".

(The lower right) "Fire weed" and "fire weed cloth". According to "Nanzhao Chronicles": "The 'fire weed' leave is about 10 or 13.5 cm long with floss on the back which is made into yarn and woven into cloth about 23.5 cm wide. It is thought to be able to get fire from making it as flint, therefore, 'fire weed' is named." The "fire weed cloth" can be made into clothes, knapsacks, bags, etc.

Young men's sleeveless jacket in Lunan

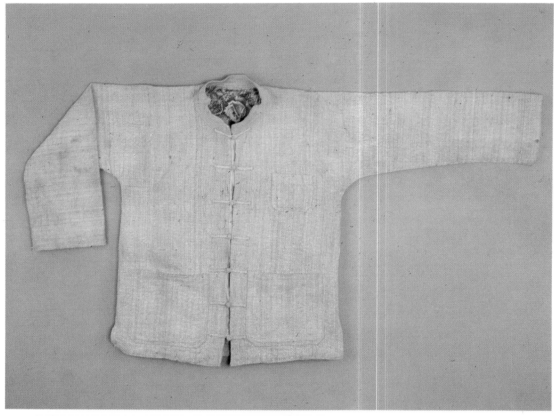

The Yi women from Lunan Guishan, Shilin, West Mile, and a part of East Mile districts like to wear clothes made of blue and white materials. The jacket reaches the knees, and the sleeves are very loose. An apron is worn with a corner folded up to the right side of the waistband. A retangular cape is worn over the left shoulder. A pair of trousers and a pair of pointed-tip embroidered shoes complete the suit.

One of the outstanding characteristics of this style of costumes is the headdress of cloth hoop. The colour and the adornment of the hoop vary with the ages and the districts. Young girls' hoop is adorned with a pair of triangular slips of embroidered colth close to the ears, and a bunch of beads hung down from the back of the head and thrown over the shoubder to the bosom. It is said that this kind of hoop was modelled after the rainbow in memory of a girl who died for love by throwing herself into fire.

Pointed-tip embroidered shoes.

Lunan women's headdress-cloth hoop. The left one is for middle-aged and old women. It is in two colours only—black and red. The right one in multicolours is for young women.

Women's jacket in Lunan.

Cape worn on the back.

Old women's attire in Shilin of Lunan.

Ancient style overall apron worn by women in Lunan. It is pieced together with coloured cloths and embroidered. It is simple and tasteful.

117

Women's attire in Qiubei. The Yi nationality here are immigrants from Guishan, and the women's attire has kept the characteristics of Guishan women's wear.

A jacket with the back longer than the front worn by the women in Qiubei. It is pieced together with big pieces of cloths in two colours.
The opening is a little to the right.

The hanging bag with bell designs used by young girls.

118

Small embroidered quilt for carrying baby on the back. The embroidery in the center is 33 cm. long and 27 cm. wide.

Handkerchief with cross-stitch work. Yi women in Lunan are very good at cross-stitch craft. A handkerchief with full cross-stitch work and full embroidery has always been used as a betrothal token between lovers.

Young Yi girls from West Mountaineous District of Mile County wearing a close-fitting jacket made of black and white or blue cloths with an oblique opening in the front. The front is shorter than the back which reaches the back of the knees. A pair of trousers with a small apron complete the suit. The front of the jacket, the cuff and the hem of the trousers are all adorned with patterns. Middle-aged women and young girls like to carry a cross-stitched satchel while the old women mostly use hanging bag made of linen thread.

Yi girl from Mile.

Women's jacket.

Women's trousers.

120

The linen-thread-hanging-bag used by old women and the cross-stitched satchel used by middle aged and young women.

Apron.

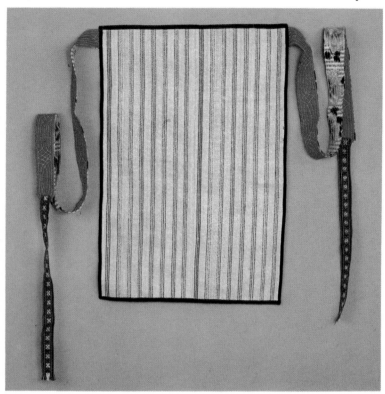

Children's cap.

Cross-stitched waistband.

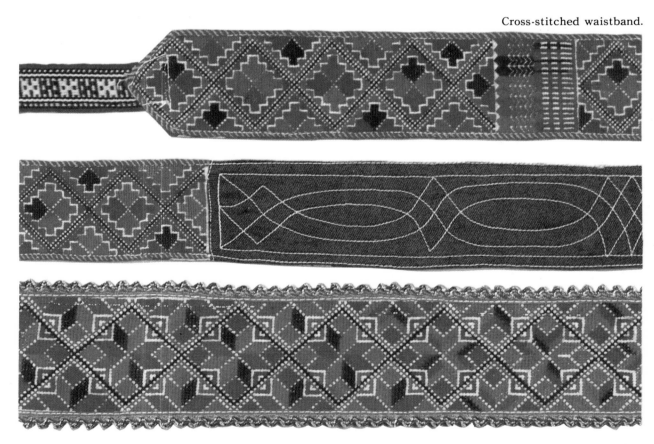

121

MILE STYLE

This style of costumes is mainly popular in Mile, Huaning, Yiliang, Luxi, Wenshan, Yanshan and Qiubei districts of Yunnan Province.

The basic style of women's attire is a jacket with buttons on the right side or down the front, a pair of trousers, an overall apron with a waistband. There are great regional differences in the colour of the women's dress, the ornaments and the headdress.

The main craft is cross-stitch work. Some Yi's wear in Luxi and Qiubei districts has a large patch of cross-stitch work. They like to cross-stitch symmetric patterns with red thread on a light coloured cloth. Part of Yi people from Mile County are especially good in meticulous twine cross-stitch work. The patterns give a stereoscopic impression.

The Yi women from Wushan, Xunjian and Jiang-bian areas of Mile county like to use blue, white and green cloths for their dresses. They decorate the sleeves, shoulders, the hems and the slits on the sides of a garment with inlaid borders. Their trousers are mostly in black with tight legs and short crotch. The bottoms of the trouser legs are edged with a piece of coloured cloth of 25cm. A piece of cloth inlaid on the crotch means the woman is married.

Girl's wear in Mile.

(left) silver-bulb hoop for headdress; silver hanging earrings and silver bracelets. (right) kerchief of 30 × 30 cm. with ribbons 100 cm. long and 4 cm. wide. It is worn on the head with one corner pointing to the forehead and the opposite corner hanging on the back of the head. Ribbons and silver chains are tied on the ker-chief and their ends fall on the back of the head.

Overall apron.

Some Yi people from Luxi, Qiubei and Mile Dongshan Districts wear a short jacket with opening on the right, a sleeveless jacket over it, and a pair of trousers. They wear aprons both in the back and in the front, and a waistband 60-70 cm. long and 20 cm. wide. There are cross-stitched patterns on the sleeveless jacket, the aprons and the waistband.

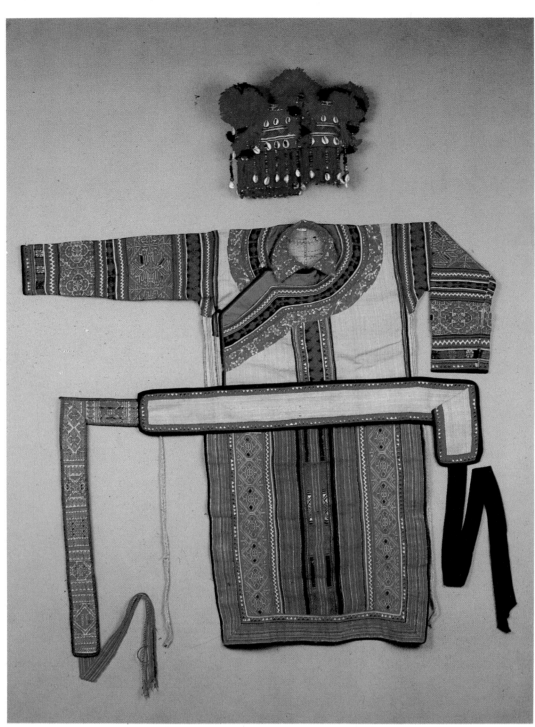

Young girls' wear in Luxi.

The back ornamental design of the sleeveless jacket worn by the women in Qiubei.

Young women's wear in Midong of Mile County.

Young girl's jacket in Dongshan District of Wenshan County.

The back of the jacket worn by the women of luxi County.

126

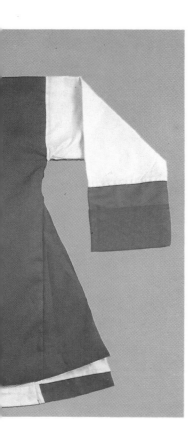

Young girls' kerchief, apron and legwear
in Dongshan District of Wenshan County.

According to historical records, the Yi people in Wushan of Mile County and Luxi were immigrants from Zhaotong during the periods of Yuan and Ming dynasties. The style of their costumes is quite different from the other Yi's in Mile. Men used to wear a long gown, a felt hat or a skullcap in blue. The men's wear now is similar to that of the local Han nationality. The women's wear varies as the age gets on. Little girls wear colourful dresses and embroidered hat decorated with long feathers. Girls, 8-16 years old wear hat that exposes the hair, colourful clothes and embroidered shoes. The grown-up women normally wear blue short jacket with a long gown and sleeveless jacket over it, an edge-decorated apron tied around the waist, and a pair of trousers with loose legs and embroidery hem. They wear silver-bulb plate headgear before marriage and hoop thereafter. The old women's wear is very simple and quiet with less ornaments.

Girls' splendid attires.

Old women's robe (outer garment) in Mile.

128

A sleeveless garment with black coarse cotton cloth as background.the front part is inlaid with silver bulbs, and the back part is decorated with embroidery.

Women's plate headgear with black coarse cotton cloth as the background and with silver bulbs decorating the front and embroidery on the back.

Overall apron.

129

WENXI STYLE

This style is mainly popular in Wenshan, Xichou, Malipo and Funing of Yunnan Province, and Napo of Guangxi Zhuang Autonomous Region.

The distinguished characteristics of this style are: The attire has kept very strong traditional colour. The ancient collarless robe is still worn by Yi people in some regions as splendid attire on festivals and ceremonial occasions. The crafts of the clothes are mainly batik and appliqueing. In Malipo and Funing of Yunnan and Napo of Guangxi, batik is applied not only to the women's dresses but also to men's wears which show quite different styles. The main designs of Malipo batik are fine rings and dots while the designs of Funing and Napo batik are mainly very daring geometric patterns.

The women's wear includes a short jacket with buttons down the front or with buttons on the right side, a pair of medium-length trousers, and a long skirt with simple adornments. The old women in Napo of Guangxi like to wear several combs in the hair as adornment and earrings as well.

The jacket, kerchief and batik skirt worn by girls in Malipo, Yunnan. The background of the dress is homewoven cloth with hidden stripes. Around the shoulder, the front openings, the cuffs of the sleeves and the lower hem of the jacket are inlaid with batik cotton prints. The skirt is also inlaid with triangular pieces of cloth in various colours.

The women of Napo on a festival. Abundance of clothes means wealth and beauty to them.

Women's waistband of Napo. It is said that is the ancient times the women soldiers wore iron hoop to protect themselves. This kind of hoop was made of soaked bark later and adorned with brocade band. This has become a custom through long usage and the hoop is only an ornament now.

132

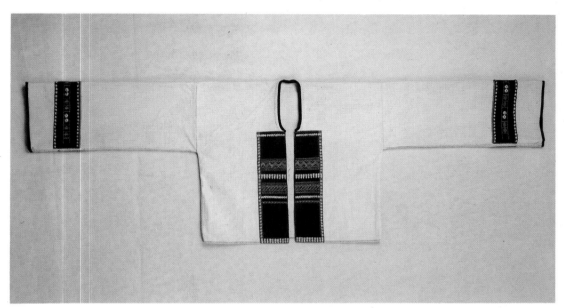

Women's jacket in Napo.

The batik robe worn by the women of Napo, Guangxi. It is collarless and buttonless, and reaches the shins. There are slits on both sides. The batik paintings on the back and the front include the designs of sun, moon and stars, and some other patterns implying good luck and propitiousness which shun evil spirit and ensure safety. Yi people call it "Dragon and Phoenix Pattern". This attire is mostly worn on festivals.

Some Yi women from Guangxi Napo and Yunnan Funing County generally wear white or blue jackets with an opening in the middle and with a few floral and silver shell adornments, and a pair of black trousers with broad legs which reach the knees with a waistband and black leggings.

133

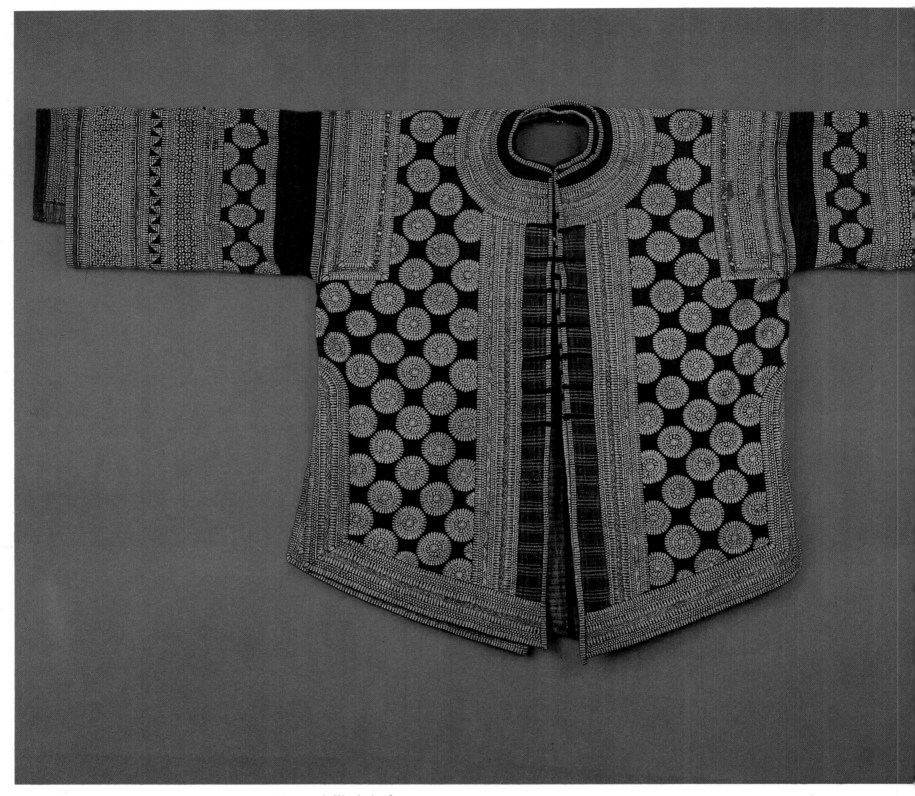

Men's batik jacket. Men who live in Malipo and Xinzhai of Yunnan Province normally wear white undershirt with slightly ornamental designed opening, a pair of black cloth trousers and a kerchief made of checked fabric. Batik jackets are worn on festivals. The wear usually consists of three jackets with the sleeves getting shorter and broader from the one inside to the one on top. The front and the back of the jackets are in angular shape. A cross-stitched broad waistband is tied over the jacket. The batik jackets are dyed and made by the bride herself as a wedding present to the bride-groom.

Lined Jacket worn by the men in Napo. This is a traditional buttonless outer coat with a front opening; the sleeves are short and broad; the upper parts of the opening are inlaid with two rows of silver-piece; and the slits on both sides and the cuffs are inlaid with white embroidered pieces.

Men with splendid attire during "Bow Dance" Festival.

The cross-stitched waistband worn by Napo men. It is made of home-woven cloth. The two ends are adorned with exquisite embroidery and tin pieces with plum blossom design. During "Bow Dance", the leading dancer wears such a waistband that tied around waist or thrown over the shoulders.

135

The wear of the Yi women from Wantang and Baihe to the east of Nanxi River of Pingbian County. The jacket reaches the waist with a small collar and opening on the right. The pleated skirt is made of black cloth and matched with a broad waistband. A bow-shape hair-frame is worn on the head covered with a kerchief, twined with embroidered band adorned with silver and glass beads, and shells.

Jacket and skirt worn by the girls in Wantang of Pingbian County.

A woman in Pingbian is spinning.

The quardruple embroidered ribbons hanging down on the back.

136

The kerchief, headband, hair-frame, headhoop and bead-tassels worn by the women of Pingbian.

The short blouse and pleated skirt worn by girls from Xichou County. The blouse is pieced together with pieces of coloured cloth in geometric patterns.

THE WEST YUNNAN MODEL

WEISHAN STYLE

JINGDONG STYLE

This model is mainly popular in the Ailao and Wuliang mountain ranges in the west of Yunnan including Dali, Simao and Lincang. It's worn by a population of 500,000 speaking a western dialect.

West Yunnan is the birthplace of ancient Nanshao, and one of the main regions where Yi nationality live in community. According to "The Chart of Tribute System of Royal Qing", during the early Qing Dynasty, in Dali and Menghua (now around Weishan) of West Yunnan, some Yi people's attire were:"The men tie their hair and wrap up their head... wear a woolen cape and a sword." They feed themselves by shooting birds and animals with wooden bows and medicated arrows. The women wrap their head with black cloth, adorned with giant clams, wear a short blouse and a long skirt, and are barefooted. Women also learn to hunt with bow and arrow." The Yi's attires around Dali of West Yunnan have changed greatly in the last 200 years.

Now, most women wear round collar jacket with opening on the right and with the back longer then the front, a pair of trousers, a sleeveless jacket and an apron. They like to wear silver ornaments. Around the mountain regions of Weishan, Midu and Dali, the women's formal costume is mostly in green or red with embroidered oversleeves richly decorated. They also wear a unique felt "guobei" (a kind of round hanging with one piece of felt sticking on top of another). They either wear cloth cap or wrap their head with a black kerchief adorned with colourful tassels and strings of beads which match beautifully with the multicoloured streamers tied around the waist. This costume reminds one of the magnificent dress and adornments worn by the ancient Nanshao royalty. The women's costumes in the adjacent mountain regions such as Jingdong, Nanjian and Nanhua are also in gorgeous colours. The women's dress in other districts are much quieter and with less adornments.　The basic style of the attire is similar to the women's dress as painted in Qing's mural "Singing under the tree" in Wenlong Pavilion on Weibao Mountain. The present costume is certainly an inheritance of the local Yi's dress in the middle and late Qing Dynasty.

The peasants in mountain area, men and women, all like to wear goatskin cape with a tail, which is an ancient custom of Yi nationality in West Yunnan.

Several decades ago, men wore a long gown with opening on the right and a pair of trousers with loose legs, and with a black kerchief wrapped round the head, as well as a waistband or a leather abdomen-cover. Now, they mostly wear modern suits of clothes. The exquisite sleeveless jacket made of chamois or goatskin is the men's favorite traditional costume in some areas.

Weishan Plain--the birthplace of Nanzhao.

The mural "Singing under the tree" of Qing Dynasty (around 1759) in the Wenlong Pavilion in Weibao Mountain. This mural vividly depicts the basic model and characterteristics of the Yi's attire in West Yunnan during the reign of Emperor Qianlong of Qing Dynasty.

WEISHAN STYLE

This model is mainly popular in Weishan, Midu, Nanjian and a part of Dali area.

The women wear a jacket with buttons on the right, a round collar and a back longer than the front with a sleeveless jacket in dark colour over it, and an apron as well. In the mountain areas of Weishan and Midu, the women wear embroidered felt "guobei" matched with splendid colourful attire. The apron is embroidered with various designs of flowers and plants. Around the area of Nanjian, the women's jacket and apron are shorter. The jacket is usually white and the trousers blue. The sleeveless jacket and the apron are black with only a little decoration on the sleeveless jacket.

The headdress varies from place to place. The girls in the east of Weishan have long plaits and wear a "fish tail" cap. They have their hair done up in a bun and wrapped with a kerchief after they get married. When they are dressed up, they wear colourful tassels and strings of beads. The girls around Nanjian and Wuliangshan wear several bunches of velvet flowers as headdress when they are in formal dress, while middle-aged and old women only wrap their head with black cloth.

Both men and women in Nanjian like to wear a buttonless and sleeveless goatskin cape. Black goatskin with very long hair is the best. Some men in Weishan also wear goatskin cape.

Men normally wear modern suits of clothes. During festivals, a vest made of cloth, chamois or goatskin is worn over the clothes.

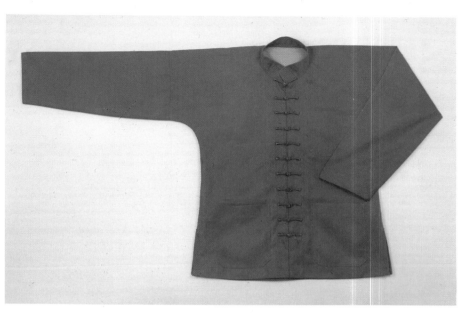

Weishan men's jacket.

Weishan men's traditional chamois vest.

A traditional goat skin cape.

Men's embroidered shoes with leather
soles handed down from ancient times.

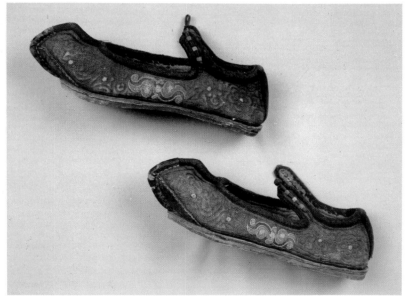

In the Yi district around west Yunnan, both men and women like to wear a goatskin cape. It is collarless, sleeveless and buttonless. It drapes naturally except a slight cut done under the armpits. The four legs and the tail of the goatskin must be kept in their natural shapes. This cape has a unique style. It is made of two pieces of goatskin. Black skin with long hair is the best. In some places, a goatskin cape is the indispensable dowry of a girl. The peasants wear it when working in the fields. When it is clear, the cape is worn with the hair facing inside, when it is rainy, with the hair facing outside. It is an especially suitable garment for high and cold mountainous areas as it can shelter one from the wind and rain and keep one warm.

Women's jacket and vest of Dongshan in Weishan. The back of the jacket reaches the back of the knees while the front reaches the waist only. It has to be worn with an apron.

Dressed-up Dongshan Yi women of Dongshan in Weishan.

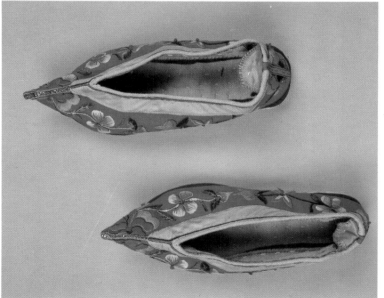

Traditional women's shoes in Wuyin District of Weishan.

Embroidered apron is an essential ornament of women's wear.

The gorgeous designs of flowers, plants, butterflies and birds are done in plain and applique embroideries.

Xishan girls' embroidered cap.

Dongshan married women's headdress.

Dongshan girl's "fish tail" cap.

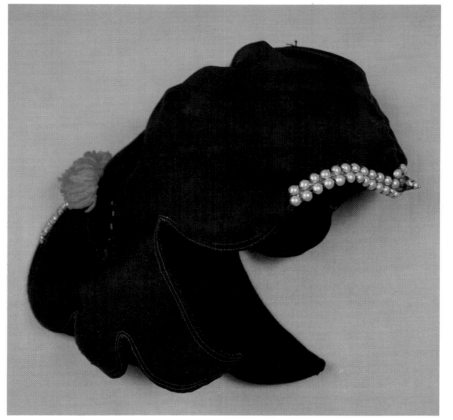

In Yi District of Weishan and Midu of Dali prefecture, and Fengyi, etc. of Dali city, the women like to wear a round felt "guobei" of 20 cm. in diameter. All the women around Dongshan of Weishan County, old and young, married or unmarried, wear "guobei". The traditional "guobei" does not have a cloth cover; but has two round figures and two rectangular figures embroidered with black thread on the white felt. In the Xishan district, the "guobei" is wrapped with a piece of black cloth on which exquisite floral designs are embroidered or inlaid.

With regard to the origin of "gubei", the story begins with the two round figures. It is said that these figures stand for spiders. Legend has it that, once upon a time, there were several girls who ran into Qinghua Cave (in the east of Dali Prefecture now) to get away from some soldiers. As soon as they entered the cave, the spiders spread webs on the entrance at once. When the pursuing troops came and saw the webs, they left. The girls were grateful to the saviouy spiders and also wanted to commemorate the narrow escape so they embroidered the spiders on the felt. Another version is that the two rectangular figures on top of the round ones are two eyes so that demons and ghosts will not dare to attack from the back. As a matter of fact, the "guobei" has the function of keeping out the cold and protecting the waist, and, it can be used as a pad when you carry a basket on your back.

The Xishan girls of Midu who wear embroidered "guobei".

The embroidered designs of "guobei" of Midu Xishan model.

Baby-suspender.

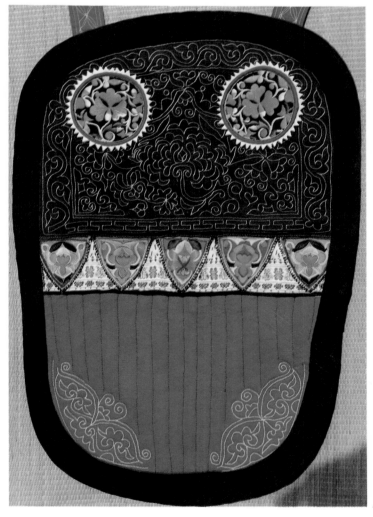

Baby carrier (band) of Ma-an-shan of Weishan.

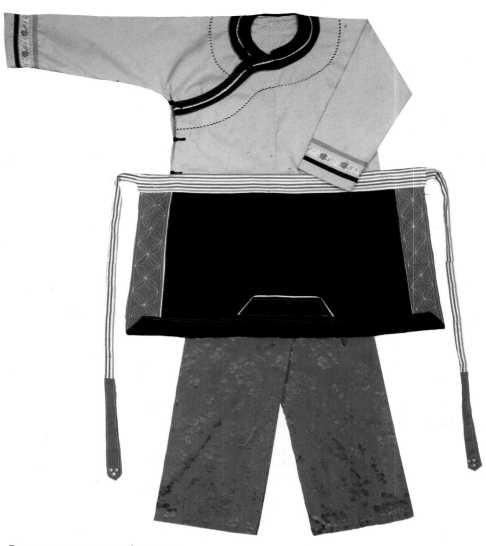

Pu-er women's everyday wear.

Jinggu women's formal attire.

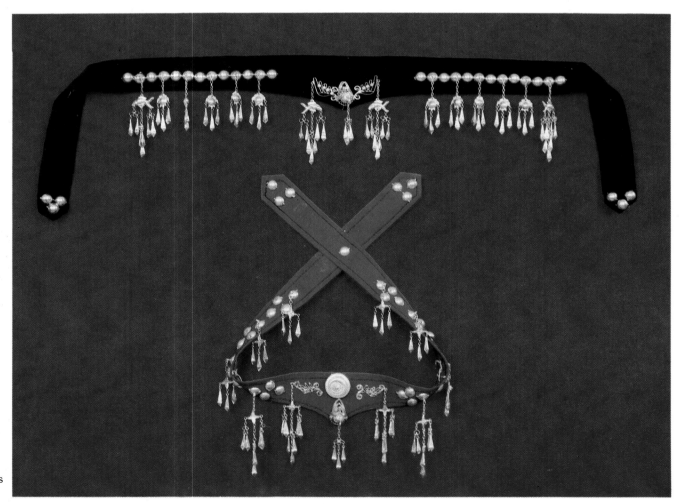

Jinggu and Pu-er women's
formal headdress.

149

Yi girls from Xinping, Eshan, Yuan-jiang and Jiangcheng of Yunnan Province have the habit of wearing a black vest with opening in the middle over the jacket. It is adorned with silver-coin buttons down the front.

Xingping women's apron with embroidery and silver ornaments.

Yongde men's jacket with opening on the right.

Jacket of Ma-an-shan girls of Weishan type. The style is not different from that of the other districts, only the floral adorn-(卍) and spirals.

A Yi woman from Ma-an-shan District of Weishan in everyday wear with a black cloth coil round the head.

Women's jacket and vest of Xishan, Midu County. The style is similar to the Dongshan Women's attire, only a little shorter.

Nanjian Yi girls in everyday wear.

Women's attire in Nanjian.

Women's shoes.

JINGDONG STYLE

This style is mainly popular in Jingdong and Jinggu of Simao District, Nanhua and Lincang of Chuxing District, and a part of Baoshan District.

Some Yi women from Jingdong and other counties like to wear a short jacket in pink or green with a black embroidered breast-apron. Other Yi women from Lincang, Baoshan, Simao and Jinggu like to wear a black or blue jacket with round shoulders. The hems of the openings are inlaid with black cloth strips in various geometric designs. The wear is simple and elegant.

There are two types of headdress. Some Yi women of Jingdong and Nanhua wear their hair in a cone wrapped in a wrapper. When they are dressed up, they wear a hairdress closely stitched with silver bulbs and several multicoloured long ribbons hanged down from the back of the head. The Yi girls of Jinggu County used to wear cocks-comb cap, In nowadays, they wear "leizi" stitched with silver flowers or wrap their head with a coloured towel. Married women wear black head-wrapper.

The traditional men's attire includes a short jacket with opening in the middle, a pair of trousers, and a head-wrapper. The clothes are mostly made of black homewoven cloth. Now, men wear modern suits, but the goatskin cape is still their favorite wear.

Women's apron in Jingdong.

Nanhua women's sleeveless jacket
with buttons down the front.

Women's hanging
bag in Nanjian.

Dressed-up women from Wuliang Region of Nanjian.

THE CHUXIONG MODEL

LONGCHUAN STYLE

DA-YAO STYLE

WUDING STYLE

This model of costume is mainly popular in Chuxiong Yi Nationality Autonomous Prefecture of Yunnan Province and its adjacent Yi districts. The population wearing this costume is about more than seven hundred thousand. Chuxiong is located between Dianchi Lake and Erhai Lake, bordered on Wumeng in the east, Jinsha in the north, and Ailao in the south, and was a center of Yi immigration in the ancient times. It is also a confluence zone of several dialects of Yi language. Therefore, the costumes are of great variety.

According to the "Chuxiong Chronicles" during the reign of Emperor Kangxi of Qing Dynasty: "Women do not wear trousers but cylindrical skirt, the jacket is not open in the front but pulled over from the head." Due to the development in economy and culture in the last hundred years, great changes have taken place in Yi's attire too. A Jacket with opening on the right and a pair of trousers have become the basic style of this model of costume worn by women. But, "all Yi people, men or women, are still keeping the old habit of wearing goatskin capes and 'fire weed' clothes, the jacket pulled over from the head and skirt at various places."

The women's jacket of this model is rather short but colourful with plenty of ornaments. The crafts generally include cross-stitch, inlaid work, insertion and embroidery. The designs are mainly flowers and plants. Designs of double square are extensively used. The traditional cloud and silk flower designs are mostly done on the breast and shoulders of the jacket.

The women's hairdress are in great variety. There are three main types: wrapper, twined kerchief, and embroidered cap. They can be calssified into more than 40 kinds, and each kind has it distinctive regional characteristics which become the mark of Yi's nationality of that place.

Men wear a short jacket and a pair of trousers. Their attire is taking after the modern style more and more.

The night of Torch Festival
in Chuxiong Yi Prefecture.

Yi nationality Village.

Da-yao Yi girls performing stamp-foot dance.

LONGCHUAN STYLE

This model of costume is mainly popular in Mouding, Chuxiong, Nanhua and Shuangbai along the Longchuan River in Chuxiong Prefecture.

The women's jacket is rather shorter and in light colour with a black vest over it. A pair of trousers and a breast-apron complete the suit. The apron is embroidered with various flowers and plants designs and geometric figures. It is the main ornament of the suit.

Women mostly wrap their head with a black kerchief into a plate shape. The headdress varies a little in different regions. Some wear their hair in a bun at the back of the head, twined with a black kerchief and the bun is adorned with silver pin and chains. Some decorate their kerchief with several colourful floss flowers, or wear headhoop fully adorned with silver flowers and bulbs.

The basic model of the men's attire includes a short jacket and a pair of trousers. The jacket is adorned with a bit of embroidered flowers. The traditional woolen cape, the jacket with opening on the right and the embroidered abdomen-cover are still worn by some middle-aged and old men. The ancient goatskin cape and the colourful embroidered sandals are young men's favourite wear.

Women from Chuxiong and Mouding wrap their head with black cloth into a round plate shape about 30 cm. in diameter. The cloth amounts to several tens of feet long and is adorned with silver flowers and tassels or colourful floss balls.

The women's dress is a jacket with opening on the right and tight sleeves. An embroidered vest mostly in a dark colour is worn over it. They also wear an embroidered overall apron with a silver chain. The women used to wear a skirt, but now they wear a pair of trousers in stead, and the embroidery is on the middle part of the trouser legs.

Yi girls of Muliu in Chuxiong

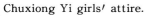

Chuxiong Yi girls' attire.

Embroidered shoes for women.

Girls' headdress in some districts of Daguokou and Shuangbai County of Chuxiong City.

The jacket and the apron.

The characteristic of the women's vest is that the front part is shorter than the back. It is always worn together with an apron.

164

Inlay, plain embroidery and cross-stitched work are combined together in decorating women's ribbons. The disigns are very simple.

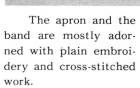

The apron and the band are mostly adorned with plain embroidery and cross-stitched work.

The traditional men's attire are mostly made of fabric of mixed wool and cotton or homewoven fabric of mixed linen and "fire weed".

The jacket is always with a right-side opening. The shoulders and sleeves are embroidered slightly with simple and elegant designs. The men's jacket in the picture here has a history of a hundred years. It is made of handwoven cloth of mixed wool and cotton.

Chuxiong Yi youth.

The men's embroidered sandals.

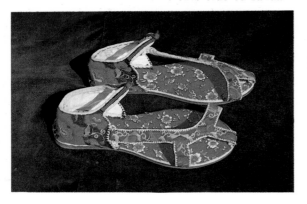

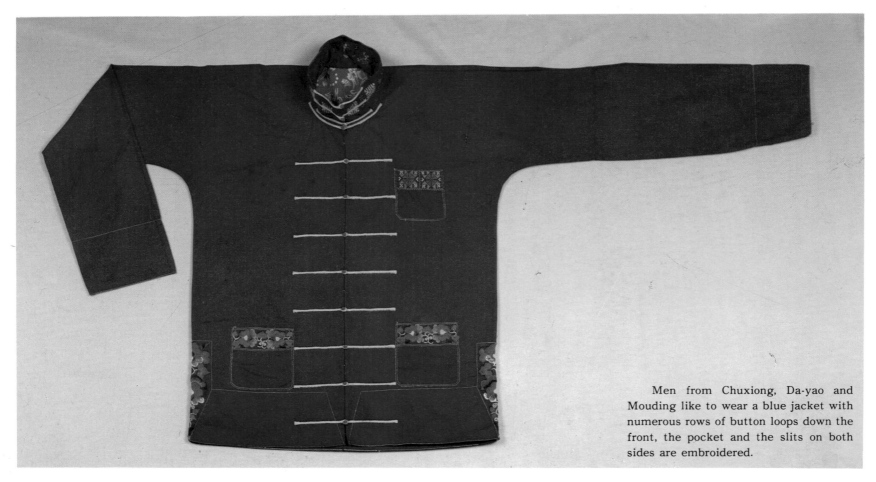

Men from Chuxiong, Da-yao and Mouding like to wear a blue jacket with numerous rows of button loops down the front, the pocket and the slits on both sides are embroidered.

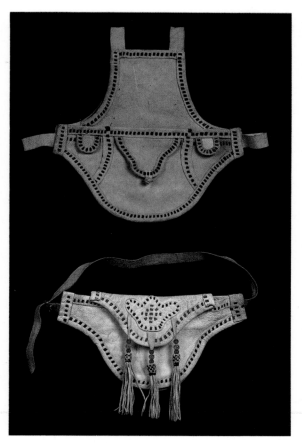

The chamois abdomen-cover is also a men's traditional ornament. It is mostly sewed with coloured leather strings. The stitches naturally form a decorative border. The workmanship is excellent. The cover is beautiful and durable.

Men's embroidered abdomen-cover is 30-55 cm. long and about 20 cm. wide. It is mostly made of black cloth embroidered with various designs which are simple, archaic and elegant. Men wear it on the bosom when they are dressed up. It is used to contain money or small articles of everyday use.

DA—YAO STYLE

This mode is mainly popular in Da-yao, Yao-an and Yongren in the northwest of Chuxiong Prefecture.

The women's attire has several styles. Some wear a jacket with right-side opening and a pair of trousers. Others wear a jacket with opening in the middle and a medium-length skirt.

The women's attire in Tanhua of Da-yao and Santai are in beautiful bright colours. The jacket is mostly made of red or blue silk or satin and inlaid with black, yellow and red laces. They also wear three embroidered aprons at the same time. They cover their head with an embroidered kerchief with colourful tassels. When the middle-aged and old women are dressed up, they also wear colourful clothes, but ordinarily they wear black. They all like the goat-skin cape. The girls wear silver eardrops.

Around Jumen and Guanglu of Yao-an, the women's jacket is short and plain, but the cloud designs on the border of the opening are very striking.

The Da-yao Guihua women's attire includes a jacket, a pair of embroidered leggings and a black embroidered skirt. The jacket is with an opening in the middle, and with a back longer than the front. Both the back and the front are inlaid with coloured cloth in various geometric patterns. The skirt is inlaid with horizontal stripes of coloured cloth. This mode is unique, bold and archaic, entirely different from all the other modes.

The girls wrap their head with an embroidered kerchief, and with a black kerchief after marriage. The kerchief for dressing-up is adorned with shells, silver flowers, silver bulbs or multi-colour long tassels. This style is handed down from the ancient times.

Da-yao women like to use chamois hanging bag, while the men wear a chamois abdomen-cover.

Da-yao women's attire.

Yao-an women's sleeveless jacket.

Da-yao cross-stitched streamers.

The various sewing kits worn by Yao-an women.

Da-yao Yi girl.

Silk flower (Mi-yi-lu in Yi language) is Yi people's favourite flower which is extensively used in decorative designs. According to legend that Mi-yi-lu was a pretty, clever shepherdess who lived in the Tanhua Mountain of Da-yao County. She gave her life for the rescue of the villagers. In the memory of her, on the day of Mi-yi-lu's death, February 8th of every lunar year, the villagers will hold a wearing-flower festival. People will stick flower on each other, and at the same time, they will stick a bunch of blossoming silk flowers on the doors and in the fields. They also adorn the ox horn and sheep horn as well as the farm implements with silk flowers.

The picture shown is the back-carrier with silk flowers design.

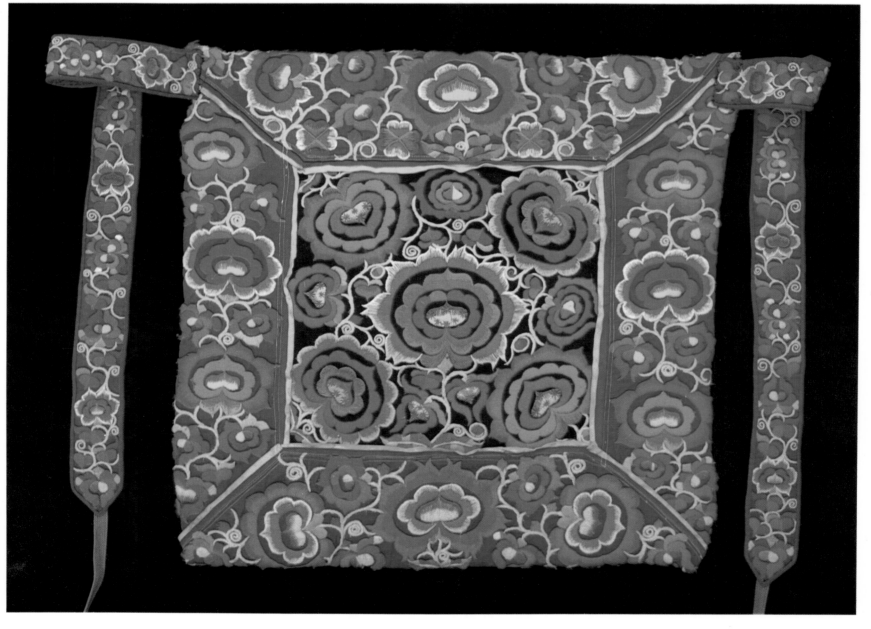

During the festivals, the girls' embroidered kerchiefs are a mass of gorgeous colours.

Embroidered kerchief is the important headdress for the women of Da-yao and Yao-an. The kerchief is mostly a square piece of black cloth, its sides are about 170 cm long each. The embroidered designs are either concentrated in one corner or dispersed in four corners. The embroidered corner should be turned to the top of the head. Some square kerchief may be fully embroidered with designs and adorned with silver chains and coloured tassels all around. Most of the designs are flowers and plants done in exquisite plain embroidery craftmanship.

173

Da-yao Guihua women's attire. This kind of attire is simple and unsophisticated, and is entirely different from the other models of Yi area. The jacket is opened in the middle without buttons. The front reaches the waist while the back reaches the back of the knees. A skirt, a pair of leggings with inlaid work and a pair of embroidered shoes complete the suit. The jacket, the skirt and the leggings, are all made with black cloth and inlaid with coloured cloth in various geometric patterns. The characteristic of this mode is the extensive application of inlaid craft.

The adornment on the back of the jacket.

174

Young men's jacket. The embroidered silk flower on the upper left pocket is the expression of a girl's best wishes signifying happiness and good luck. The embroidered tigers on the two lower pockets mean tiger-worship.

Young men from Yao-an and Da-yao.

Cross-stitched hanging bag of Da-yao style.

WUDING STYLE

This model is mainly popular in the counties of Wuding, Lufeng, Yongren, Yuanmou, Shuangbai in the east of Chuxiong Prefecture, the counties of Luquan, Fumin under the administration of kunming City and Xundian County of Qujing.

The basic style of this mode consists of a jacket with right opening, a pair of trousers and an apron. The girls' formal attire is fully embroidered. Around the shoulder, there is a row of colourful fringes or silver tassels. There is about a piece of 60 cm floral adornment on the bottoms of the trouser legs. The exquisite cross-stitched human figures are the most distinguishing features. The adornment of the women's attire varies from place to place. The different girls' caps become the mark of the women's attire of different places, such as the "parrot beak" cap of Wuding County, the "butterfly" cap of Lufeng County, and the "oriental cherry" cap of Yuanmou County, etc.

In some districts of Wuding and Lufeng counties, the girls wear traditional "fire weed" cape, and in Luquan and Xundian counties, they still keep the ancient habit of wearing the collarless pull-over garment.

The embroidered adornment around shoulders.

Young girls' attire (Wuding and Lufeng styles)

177

The girls' attire of Maojie of Wuding; Zhongcun of Lufeng; and Huatong of Yuanmou; are decorated with embroidered round figures around the shoulders, on the front opening and the back of a jacket and on the "fire weed" cape. The "fire weed" cape is cleverly designed and meticulously embroidered, and is the unique adornment for this mode. The middle-aged and old women like to wear a goat skin cape.

The old women's attire in Maojie of Wuding.

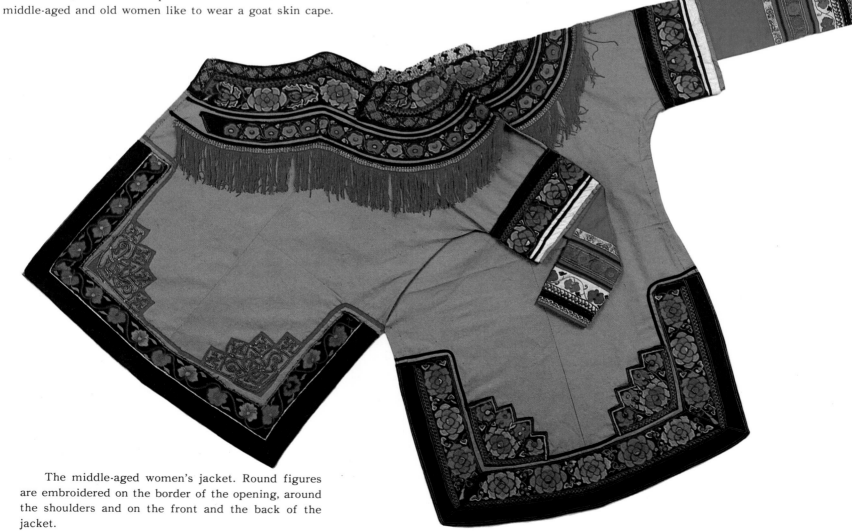

The middle-aged women's jacket. Round figures are embroidered on the border of the opening, around the shoulders and on the front and the back of the jacket.

178

"Fire weed" is a perennial wild herbaceous plant extensively growing all over the Yi districts. Its leave is about 20 cm long, with strong and tough fibre. In ancient times, it was used as the kindling of fire. thus the name, "fire wed". People in Yi districts used to spin and weave with "fire weed" fibre, and the cloth was the main material for dresses. Since the "fire weed" cloth is durable and warm and humidity-proof, it is still popular with the people. The picture is the "fire weed" shawl.

"Fire weed" sleeveless garment.

The loom for weaving "fire weed" cloth.

179

In Huanzhou and Bailu of Wuding; Huatong of Yuanmou; Tanglang and Yunlong of Luquan; Luomian and Zhebei of Fumin, the women wear a jacket of three-quarter length. They like to embroidered the "railing" pattern. The crafts are mainly plain embroidery and inlaid work. There are three or four lines of laces around the shoulders. The women also wear an embroidered breast-apron and tied with a silver chain. There is a broad border of floral adornment at the bottom of the trouser legs with the exquisite cross-stitched designs as the most outstanding characteristic. All of the unmarried women wear a "parrot beak" cap, while the middle-aged and old women twine a black kerchief around their head.

Women's attire in Wuding.

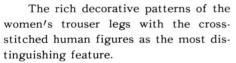

The rich decorative patterns of the women's trouser legs with the cross-stitched human figures as the most distinguishing feature.

Apron with silver chain and embroidered adornment.

180

Girls from Lufeng, wearing "butterfly" cap:

This cap is popular in Wuding and worn by middle-aged and old women. It is embroidered in patterns of dragon, phoenix and "Eight Diagrams".

The "parrot beak" cap and the "fish tail" cap with exquisite embroidery and beautiful designs.

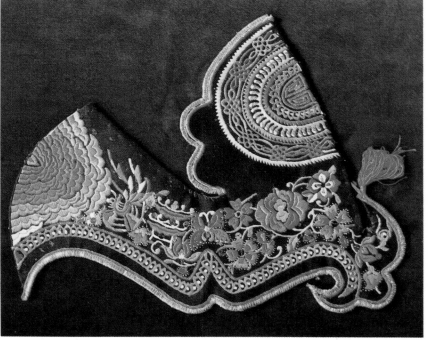

The dressed-up old women choosing embroidery patterns on the day of the Attire-competition Festival (Yongren).

In the Zhiju district of Yongren County, girls of six or seven years old up to old women of sixty to seventy, all wear a cockscomb cap, an embroidered jacket and trousers, an embroidered apron and a pair of floral shoes. This is a custom of this district only.

Yi girls from Yuanmou like to wear "oriental charry" cap.

"Inlay" is the most extensively applied traditional craft in Yi attire. It has a simple but elegant style. The patterns are characterized by vivid artistic exaggeration. The pair of birds on the apron (upper right) and the fish and bird pattern around the shoulders (lower right), both are very typical.

Cross-stitch is also a traditional craft of Yi attire. It is mostly used to adorn trouser legs and the apron of this mode of costumes and it is usually coordinated with the plain embroidery and inlaid work. It has a highly ornamental quality. The dancing human figures of Wuding are especially vivid with a unique feature.

The dressed-up Yi girls of Xundian Bangiao.

The pull-over garment is a kind of ancient wear. It was recorded in "Yunnan Chronicles" and "Chuxiong Chronicles" (in the reign of Emperor Kangxi, Qing Dynasty). The main characteristics of the garment are: "The front and the back of the women's garment are adorned with floral designs. The front does not cover the shin, the hem is curved like a tail of a banner, the upper part has a hole like the mouth of a well which is used for pulling over. The cylindrical skirt is closely pleated." This mode of costume is mainly popular in the mountainous areas among the counties of Xundian, Luquan, Songming, Shizong and Luoping.

The women's formal attire and ornaments are somewhat over-elaborate. In addition to the pull-over garment, one also wears underneath a short buttonless jacket with a front opening and colourful sleeves. On top of the garment one wears a buttonless and sleeveless jacket made of black coarse cloth with an opening in the middle. The skirt is made of red and blue coarse cloth with close pleats. A felt apron completes the suit. When it is cold, a felt cape is worn over the pull-over garment.

The pull-over garment.

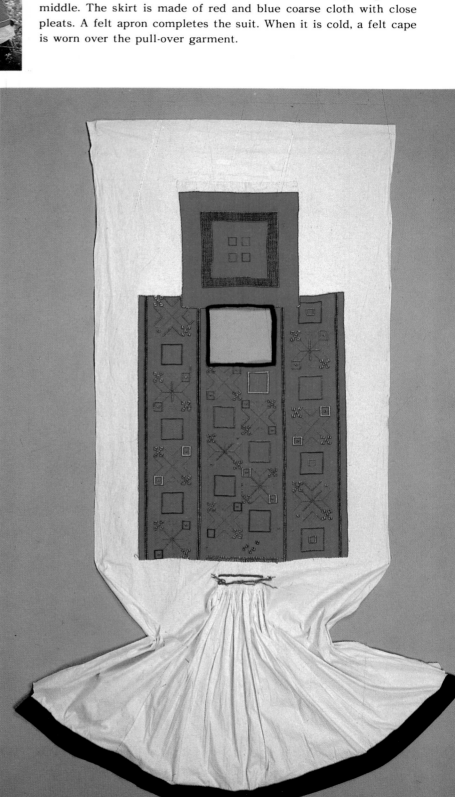

Close-pleated coarse cloth skirt with about 100 pleats.

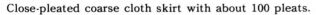

Men's jacket (Luquan style).

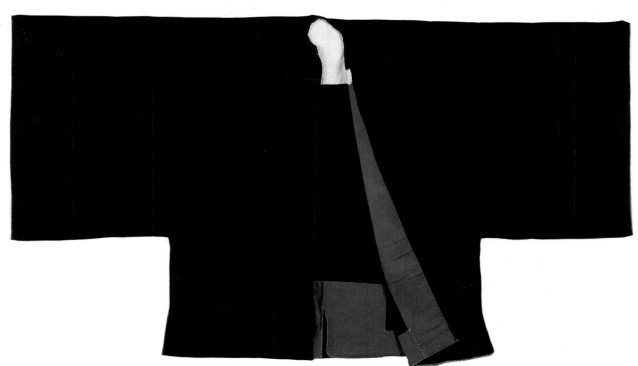

Men's sleeveless jacket.
Men's trousers.

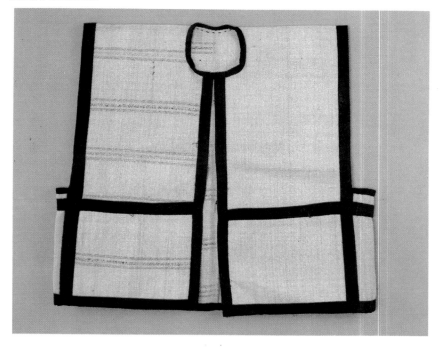

The men's jacket is loose and rather short with an opening in the middle and no button. It is mostly made of homewoven and homedyed black coarse cotton cloth. The men's trousers are made of white linen with about 60 cm wide trouser legs. When going out, a man wears a linen gown with an opening in the middle and no button. He twines a black kerchief round his head.

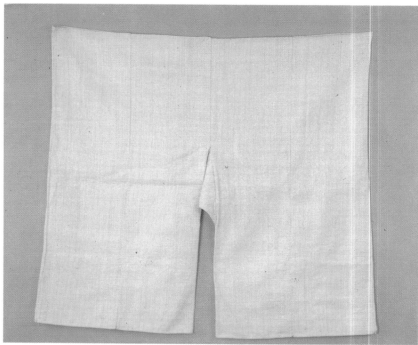

185

Yi women in some areas of Luquan and Wuding are fond of wearing red knitting wool cap which looks unique.

Silver earrings.

Silver cap-ornaments.

Silver bracelets.

Women in Yi districts usually embroider a tiger on the back-carrier, the clothes and other daily articles. Among the unearthed artifacts of Yi districts, one usually finds many tiger designs or stone tigers. There is a habit of drapping a piece of tiger fur or planting a flag with a tiger figure during the funeral ceremony or ceremony of offering sacrifice to ancestors. The world view of the universe and all things on earth being made by the disintegated tiger is also reflected in "Meige", a well known Yi epic. It is thus clear that the tiger embroidery today is originated from the longstanding tiger-worship in Yi history, and from the totem-worship of ancient Yi nationality. The tiger-head cap, tiger-head abdomen cover and tiger-head shoes which are very popular now, all imply tiger-worship.

Cross-stitched taiji design of eight tigers around the four sides.

The four-tiger design on the hanging bag.

Children's tiger-head cap.
Children's tiger-head shoes.

POSTSRIPT

Rich and colourful costumes and adornments of Yi Nationality are an important component of the brilliant culture of Yi people. In order to inherit and carry forward the fine cultural tradition of Yi Nationality, to further national cultural exchange, and to promote national unity, Beijing National Cultural Palace, Liangshan Yi Nationality Autonomous Prefecture in Sichuan Province, Chuxiong Yi Nationality Autonomous Prefecture in Yunnan Province, Hani and Yi Nationality Autonomous Prefecture in Honghe and Bijie Region in Guizhou Province organized a leading group for "Exhibitions of the Costumes and Adornments of Yi Nationality " in April, 1986. The members of the leading group are Shi Songshan (Yi), Luo Kaiwen (Yi), Yang Litian (Hui), Long Xiuhan (Miao), Zhang Fumin (Monggol), Wu Jingzhong (Yi), Liesuoziha (Yi), Qi Jinfu (Yi), Chen Wenxing (Hani), Chen Changyou (Yi), Gao Zongyu, Wang Xuefang (Yi) and Jimubuchu (Yi). Since then, the leading group and its staff have carried on a widespread and profound research on the costumes and adornments of Yi Nationality and collect samples. "Exhibitions of the Costumes and Adornments of Yi Nationality" have been held in Beijing, Guizhou, Sichuan and Yunnan Provinces since the autumn of 1987 and "The Costumes and Adornments of Chinese Yi Nationality Picture Album" is compiled on the basis of these exhibitions.

In the preparation of exhibitions and the compilation of the album, we got warmly support and help from Sichuan, Yunnan, Guizhou Provinces and Guangxi, regional nationalities affairs commissions, cultural departments, Lunan and Weishan Yi Nationality Autonomous Counties and many Yi cadres and broad masses of Yi people. The leaders of State Nationalities Affairs Commission showed every concern towards our work. We also wish to extend our thanks to Feng Yuanwei, Long Zhiyi, Li Guiying, Bai Kui, Sun Ziqiang, Lu Wenbin, Huang Meixian, Na Shihua, Liu Yaohan, Yang Tianshou, Xu Yongyi, Zhang Wugu, Liu Zhiqing and Tang Chuiyu who gave us a lot of support and help.

Yi Nationality is distributed over a vast area and its costumes and adornments are numerous and colourful. It is hard to avoid omissions in the collection of costumes and the compilation of the album, we hope our readers will oblige us with valuable comments.

（京）新登字 210 号

图书在版编目（CIP）数据

中国彝族服饰/彝族服饰编委会编. —北京：北京工艺美
术出版社，1994.4
ISBN 7-80526-033-8

Ⅰ．中…　　Ⅱ．彝…　　Ⅲ．服饰-中国-彝族-画册
Ⅳ.K829.23

中国版本图书馆 CIP 数据核字（94）第 02129 号

中国彝族服饰　（英文版）

中国彝族服饰画册编写组编

北京工艺美术出版社出版
（北京市东城区沙滩后街 30 号　邮政编码 100009）
民族印刷厂印刷
中国国际图书贸易总公司发行
（中国北京车公庄西路 35 号
北京邮政信箱第 399 号　邮政编码 100044）

1990 年 6 月第 1 版
1994 年 5 月第 2 版第 1 次印刷　（英文版）
ISBN 7-80526-033-8/G・14
　　　15000（精）
　　　84-E-739 D

中华人民共和国印刷

First Printing 1990
Second Printing 1994
ISBN 7-80526-033-8/G · 14

Published by: Beijing Arts and Crafts Publishing House
Printed by: Nationalities Printing House
Distributed by: China International Book Trading Corporation
35 Chegongzhuang Xilu, Beijing 100044,
China P. O. Box 399, Beijing, China